CW00801499

freedom is
my religion

PAT CONDELL
freedom is my religion

Copyright © Pat Condell 2012

All Rights Reserved. No part of this publication may be
reproduced or transmitted in any form or by any means,
electronic or mechanical, including photocopy, recording or
any other information storage and retrieval system, without
prior permission in writing from the author.

First published in 2012 by www.lulu.com

ISBN: 978-1-291-19783-9

www.patcondell.net

Contents

Introduction

Hello again. If you've read my first book you'll know what to expect from this one. It contains the transcripts of fifty-eight video monologues posted on the internet between November 2009 and November 2012, dealing mainly with religion, multiculturalism, and a bit of politics – or a lot of politics, depending on your point of view.

My argument with religion has always been political, not metaphysical. I don't care what anyone believes about reality as long as they keep it away from me. Yes, I'm an atheist, but I could be wrong about that. For me, the existence or otherwise of God is not the most pressing issue on the planet right now, not by a long way.

For the record, I don't condemn anyone who gets personal fulfilment from their religion any more than I do someone who finds meaning in astrology or tarot cards. However, people who are into astrology and tarot cards don't, as a rule, claim a spurious moral authority to force their beliefs and values into the lives of others or to inflict them on millions of children before their minds are fully formed, and that's where my problem with religion starts.

Over the last few years I've come to regard freedom as my personal religion because, thanks to the politics of both religion and the self-styled progressive left (which is actually regressive and instinctively authoritarian), we are now less free than we were a few decades ago. Freedom of speech is being squeezed into ever narrower parameters and we're lying to ourselves about it; we pretend we live in a free society, yet we can be arrested for having the wrong opinion. Democracy can no longer change the course of our destiny; we can vote all we like, but the course has been set, and all we can do is change one self-serving crew for another. And worst of all, in turning a blind eye to the fundamental misogyny of Islam, we're behaving as if the rights of women are negotiable.

People often accuse me (rather disingenuously, I think) of focusing too much on Islam and not enough on other religions, when it should be obvious even to the dimmest among them that other religions don't deserve the same focus because other religions don't promote violent jihad, other religions don't demand death for apostates and homosexuals or advocate the massacre of Jews, other religions don't regard non-believers as lesser human beings who must be subjugated or killed, and other religions are not always crowing about how one day they will dominate the world.

It's always dangerous when religion and politics mix, and in Islam they are one and the same; the religion is political and the politics are religious, and both are anti-democracy, anti-freedom, and anti-western civilisation. Wouldn't you say that deserves a little attention?

Christianity, on the other hand, has been tamed in a way that Islam hasn't, and although it might still threaten our mental wellbeing, it no longer threatens our freedom.

I don't want to be too critical of Islam here because I don't want to be arrested as a criminal for having an opinion, so let me put this as diplomatically as possible: I believe Islam is the most dangerous and divisive force on the face of the earth, and if we continue to appease and accommodate its ugly backward values our children and grandchildren will be less free than we are, and it will be our fault.

Over the last two decades we've seen our fundamental rights systematically eroded in the name of tolerance and respect for an ideology that shows no tolerance and absolutely no respect. Indeed, it shows open contempt for other beliefs and values.

Nobody who has even glanced at the Koran can possibly regard Islam as a religion of peace. It's clearly a religion of political conquest and domination, of darkness, of the sword. It's all about submission and obedience. Peace doesn't come into it.

As for enlightenment, don't make me laugh. Islam's purpose is not to expand the human consciousness but to compress it, to block avenues of inquiry and perception, to limit the human experience, and to threaten anyone who opposes it with death.

Islam doesn't preach universal brotherhood. It preaches universal Islamic domination. There is no "love thy neighbour" or "seek the kingdom of heaven within". Instead, it's Muslims against the world, don't take infidels as friends, and try to force your religion down everybody's throat as soon as you're strong enough to do so.

As a consequence, the more I hear Muslims demanding respect for their religion, the less respect I have for it (and I started out with zero, so you can imagine where we are now). I'm not saying Muslim people don't deserve respect as human beings; of course they do, and I'll fight anyone who says different. But the fundamental beliefs and values of Islam are entirely incompatible with the core western principles of freedom and democracy (which is, I suspect, why so many western politicians love pandering to Islam; their values are also incompatible with freedom and democracy, as anyone who lives in the European Union knows only too well).

Islamic values are so aggressively non-negotiable that I think we have a duty to our children to ensure that our values are also non-negotiable, especially when it comes to women. Islam's treatment of women should be an absolute red line for every civilised person on the planet. There should be no "bridge-building", no "respectful dialogue", no "cultural awareness", no "religious sensitivity", and absolutely no attempt at "mutual understanding" until Islam moves out of the Bronze Age and starts treating women as equal in every way, so that they can dress how they like, go wherever they like, and behave any way they choose without any interference at all from men.

It's hard not to notice that one group of people who have been conspicuously silent about Islam's brutalisation of women are "progressive" western feminists who apparently have more important issues to deal with, like sexist language and innuendo in the workplace.

A handful of feminists do speak out about Islamic misogyny because they've written to me and told me so, and I'm very happy to hear it, but there are many more who stay silent, and who even defend Islam, because "all cultures are equal and we shouldn't be so arrogant and blah blah blabbity blah..."

It's quite perverse and astonishingly self-absorbed. It's as if black people were making a point of respecting someone's right to hold black slaves to show how enlightened they are. Feminism will take a long time to live this one down. No amount of back-pedalling and revisionism in the future is going to change the cold hard fact that two thousand young girls are genitally muti-lated every year in the UK alone and nothing is done about it; we have honour killings, forced marriages and sharia courts where women are treated as half human, and every day we hear stories of women tortured, murdered, mutilated and raped in the Islamic world – it must be an effort of will to ignore them all. Yet what do we get from "progressive" western feminists? Relativism, wind and tumbleweed. It's the ultimate abdication of responsibility, and it's deeply shameful.

They're not the only ones, of course. Islam doesn't get any-where near the criticism it deserves in general because people are afraid of it. I'm always hearing from people who thank me for speaking out because they're too scared to do it themselves. No other religion has that effect on people, and no religion should be allowed to have that effect on anybody in a civilised society. But it is. Publishers won't even touch certain books now because they know there'll be a violent backlash from Muslims. Anyone who dares to criticise Islam publicly can expect an avalanche of semi-literate death threats (see my website), if not a visit from the police.

In several European countries people have been convicted as criminals for simply telling the truth about this religion and for repeating what Islamic preachers themselves say about it.

Here in Britain, if you burn a copy of the Koran or spray graffiti on the wall of a mosque you'll go to prison. If you burn any other book, including the Bible, or deface any other building, including a church, you won't.

Muslim fanatics in the West have learned that if you threaten peace-loving people with violence they'll back down, censor themselves, look for compromise, try to be reasonable. In short, they'll show weakness. They'll falsely assume the same standards of decency and fairness in their aggressors as they cultivate in themselves, and that will be their undoing.

I call it the Scandinavia syndrome because it has already scarred northern Europe perhaps beyond repair, with violent "multicultural" Islamic ghettos in what used to be virtually crime-free cities, women and gay people no longer safe on the streets, anti-Semitism openly oozing from under the veneer of civilisation, and an indigenous population seemingly paralysed in a state of glassy-eyed multiculti denial.

Norway has been so "culturally enriched" by Islamic immigration it's now the anti-Semitism capital of Europe. Last year Sweden was declared the rape capital with more than twice as many rapes as anywhere else.

Since posting the video *Goodbye Sweden* I've heard from many Swedish people who lament what's happening to their country, but who feel powerless to say or do anything about it because the multiculti lie is so strong and the social pressure so great they'd rather be tasered than be called a racist or an Islamophobe. In other words they'd rather silently watch their tolerant and civilised society evaporate before their eyes than suffer the horror of being falsely called an unpleasant name. An impartial observer (and I won't pretend to be one) might say they deserve everything they get. And maybe they do, but their children don't.

Nevertheless, the Swedes look destined to become victims of their own legendary reasonableness. They want to treat people decently and they don't want to make a fuss. What chance have they got against Islam? They're wide open. Of course their country is going down the plughole. It's already circling the drain. It's only a matter of time, surely, before they remove the cross on their flag because it offends Muslims. Or maybe Norway will beat them to it to get brownie points with Hamas. Place your bets.

I'm no stranger to criticism, but some of these videos have ruffled feathers in ways I didn't expect.

I've always been criticised by left-wing atheists for my political views (as if anyone who believes in the non-existence of deities must be a socialist) but this turned from a trickle to a torrent in the May 2010 UK general election when I urged people to vote for the small political party that most closely matched their views, as the main parties have shown that they can't be trusted to reflect the will of the people who elected them.

I explained that, as nobody else was offering democratic self-determination as an option, I would be voting for the UK Independence Party, a moderate right-of-centre party opposed to Britain's membership of the European Union, an issue I believe to be the most important one facing our country.

7

I honestly thought it was a sensible and reasonable position (I still do), so I was a little surprised by the almost comical level of hostility it provoked from left-wing atheists spitting out their cornflakes to call me a fascist and a Nazi.

I was told in all seriousness that I had betrayed something called the "atheist community" and was no longer fit to be a member. People posted videos on YouTube denouncing me as a traitor. You could almost see the steam coming out of their ears.

I was used to being called a racist for criticising the religion of phoney grievance and permanent offence, but now I became a right-wing xenophobic nationalistic bigot as well. People went out of their way to deliberately connect me with the racist British National Party and began slandering me as a white supremacist (they're still doing it) when, in fact, I'm a civilisation supremacist, regardless of colour or anything else, and I've stated publicly that I'd rather drive a garden fork through my own foot than vote for the BNP.

I can only refer those people who call me a racist to the contents of this book and my previous one, *Godless and Free*. They contain every word I have ever uttered on video, so anyone who thinks I'm a racist now has the opportunity, and (I think) the duty, to prove it.

Another video that got a hostile reception was *No Mosque at Ground Zero*. This angered a lot of American liberals who were quick to cite the First Amendment and freedom of religion. And I might have agreed with them if I believed the intention was simply to build an innocent place of worship, if there was no sinister background and no triumphalist symbolism in the plan to build near Ground Zero, or if the front man with the syrupy words wasn't a secret supremacist who said one thing to American audiences and another to the Muslim world when he thought nobody was listening.

I don't dispute their legal right to build the wretched mosque (or "community centre") but I made the video because I believe the underlying motive for choosing such a site was opportunistic, malicious and deliberately disrespectful in the most breathtakingly crass and insensitive way imaginable. I believe it was a crude attempt to drive a wedge into American society by maneuvering people into a situation where they were faced with an impossible choice between their constitutional principles and standing up for themselves, and, First Amendment or not, it needed to be said. And it seems that many Americans agreed with me. At the time of writing, the video has been viewed more than six million times on YouTube alone, three quarters of those in the United States.

For a while, it seemed that every video I made got somebody hopping mad about something, and the apoplexy needle flew right off the meter briefly in August 2010 (and I lost two thousand YouTube subscribers in one day) for *An Irish Joke*, in which I responded to a news story about a humourless Irishman who got thousands in compensation for hurt feelings when somebody told him a harmless joke. Apparently, in making the video, I managed to be racist against myself, a feat of which I'm still proud.

Things took an altogether nastier turn in July 2011 when a madman committed mass murder in Norway, and my inbox immediately filled with gloating accusations of complicity, including one from a former acquaintance who got in touch after two decades to tell me I had blood on my hands.

Shortly after this I managed to alienate some of my left-wing pals from the comedy circuit when I criticised the feral scum who trashed their own neighbourhoods in the English riots of 2011.

"Why blame the victims?" I was asked indignantly. "Why not the real culprits, the bankers and their establishment friends who bailed them out at our expense?"

The riots, I was told, were caused by the state of the economy and the lack of opportunity for youngsters, and, since the bankers are responsible for screwing the economy, the riots are their fault.

Yeah, right.

It subsequently emerged that three quarters of the "youngsters" arrested in the riots had previous criminal records with an average of fifteen offences each, and a quarter had already been in prison. So, not victims then, but scum. And scum got a result, because now scum has a brand new plasma TV sitting in pride of place among all the empty pizza cartons, beer cans and chips trodden into the carpet.

However, all this nonsense was a mere prelude to the tsunami of hostility I received for speaking up for Israel, a country for which I've always had a soft spot since spending time there in my youth (more of that later).

I used to be quite critical of Israel because, like most people, I approached the situation emotionally (it's the easiest thing in the world to do) and it seemed to me that the Palestinians were getting a raw deal. Also, I didn't like the Israelis hanging on to Jerusalem for what seemed purely religious reasons.

However, the more I watched the behaviour of the two sides, the more obvious it became that one side wanted peace and the other didn't. I saw how the Palestinian leadership were given countless opportunities for a lasting and prosperous peace and rejected them all, while their people remained in misery.

The more I listened to their words and to their repeated assertion that they will never accept a Jewish state, and the more I watched Arab TV clips on the internet showing tiny children being shamelessly brainwashed into crude Jew-hatred, and the more I heard Arab clerics repeat the Koranic exhortation to wipe out the Jews (the Koran doesn't mention Palestine), the clearer it became that their fundamental problem is not with Israelis, but with Jews, and that if Israel was anything but a Jewish nation there would have been peace long ago.

I realised that the two-state solution of which I used to be in favour is actually impossible because Arab scripture-based hatred of Jews is so great that, from their febrile perspective, the only acceptable solution is complete annihilation. In short, they won't be happy until every Jew in the Middle East is dead.

So the violence and the bloodshed will never stop, no matter what the Israelis do, no matter what they agree to concede. If they gave up a hundred Jerusalems it wouldn't be enough. The Arabs would still be firing rockets over the border every day, using their own people as human shields, and we in the West would still be paying for it.

I changed my view about Israel because I realised that the Israelis are not dealing with a rational enemy they can negotiate with, but with a vicious supremacist ideology that hates Jews for who and what they are, not for where they are. One day the useful idiots of the European left will realise this too, and they'll blush for the position they hold today.

In the meantime, they're not on Israel's side (yet), but Israel is very much on their side (only they're too stupid to know it) because Israel, a country with eight million people, is second only to the United States in technological innovation – ahead of China, ahead of Russia, ahead of everybody. So, whenever one of those Palestine solidarity halfwits sends a text or a tweet about boycotting Israel, they're using Israeli technology. Maybe they should write a letter.

I've lost count of the number of supposedly liberal people who have lectured me on how intolerant I am, then told me in the next breath they hope I get prosecuted for hate speech. The truth is I don't hate anybody, not even clergy, not even terrorists, not even Swedish "journalists" (though I admit that is a close one), because I know that hate always consumes the hater; it's always ugly, and I want no part of it.

Ironically, it seems I'm a lot more liberal than my "liberal" critics because, unlike them, I don't want to see anybody prosecuted for hate speech, not even genuine haters. I know enough about human nature to know that once free speech becomes selective they can shut anybody up, bigots and their critics alike, as people in several western countries have already found out.

A number of my critics have told me they used to like my videos until, as they put it, I shifted politically to the right. However, this is far from the truth. Politically, I'm very much in the broad middle ground. Like most people, I'm liberal about some things and conservative about others. It's just that, whereas I used to default to the left, I now default to the right because I've been given no choice by the behaviour of the left, which I no longer trust or respect.

Back in the 1980s I was very much on the left. I was a card-carrying member of the Labour Party, and I was always doing benefit shows for left-wing causes, notably for the miners when their hardcore socialist leader took on the Thatcher government in a battle he was never going to win, and destroyed his industry in the process.

Throughout my stand-up career I did benefits for left-wing groups like the Socialist Workers and the Communists, as well as for CND, Amnesty International, individual Labour MPs, community action groups, housing co-ops, you name it. (I even did some for a group of anarchists who, I heard later, used the money to buy themselves a nice house in the Lake District – and good luck to them, too, cheeky sods.)

So now, when I get angry emails from idealistic young lefties who call me dude and tell me to get a life and stop being such a fascist bigot, I sympathise to some extent because I used to share their utopian certainties and half-baked assumptions about fairness and equality. I used to believe that left-wing politics would lead to a kind of social liberation, and I even carried on pretending to believe it for a long time after I knew in my heart it wasn't true. However, in the last few years I've been forced to stop denying the evidence and to acknowledge the unpleasant truth that the left is primarily about coercion and control, not liberty.

The most sinister aspect of the left is that, by corrupting the language and calling itself progressive, it has managed to create a false consensus that its envy and control-driven values are innately virtuous, while values that espouse individual freedom and responsibility are somehow immoral, and their holders deserve to be slandered as fascists. However you dress it up,

13

though, there is no virtue in a lie, and the buzzwords of the left – fairness, equality, diversity, tolerance and, above all, progressive – are lies.

Leftist statism is about as "progressive" as a typewriter; "fairness" and "equality" have been reduced to euphemisms for self-righteous envy and small-minded authoritarianism; "diversity" is to be celebrated, except when it comes to the only diversity that really matters, diversity of opinion; and as for "tolerance", I've noticed it's always leftists who demand more censorship and try to get opposing views silenced, it's always leftists who refuse to share a platform with people whose views they disapprove of, and it's always leftists who rush to excuse the intolerance and bigotry, the misogyny, homophobia and anti-Semitism of Islam – especially the hard left, which in my opinion is the nearest thing in politics to batshit crazy, displaying all the delusional knuckle-dragging righteousness of jihad without the mumbo-jumbo.

I still believe in certain left-wing principles like socialised medicine and public ownership of transport and utilities, but some things are more important, and, for me, the political left has shown its hand in so many ways that only a fool could be blind to it. Whether it's the multiculturalism and diversity lie, the fairness and equality scam, the culture of offence and phoney victimhood, the open-border Euro democracy hijack, or the deliberate injection of a backward totalitarian religion into a society where it isn't welcome and doesn't belong, the left has shown beyond any doubt that it cannot be trusted with our freedom. And freedom is my religion. (Did I mention that?)

I should emphasise that most of the mail I get is very positive and supportive. However, some of it does have a disquieting air of resignation about it. Many people tell me they're worried about the creeping Islamisation, the erosion of democracy and the crippling political correctness that's destroying the language and turning us into a society of victims and crybabies, and they ask: "But what can I do to change it?"

To which I can only reply: You can change the world around you by speaking your mind and telling the truth as you see it, unvarnished and unapologetically, regardless of who claims to be offended. If we all did that, the world would soon be a different place, and it has to start somewhere.

And here's the good news. Despite what the sensitivity and diversity industry would have you believe, other people's feelings are not more important than yours. (I know. It's a revelation, isn't it?)

Feelings are subjective, and subjectivity has a way of quickly becoming self-indulgent, so if you let other people's feelings dictate what you can say, then soon you won't be able to say anything at all; nobody will know what you think, and nobody will know or care who you are.

Didn't Gandhi say you must be the change you want to see in the world? (When he wasn't making snide cracks about western civilisation he could talk a lot of sense.)

It's true you might lose a few friends by speaking your mind, but believe me, you're well rid of them. Anyone who has a problem with your honest opinion was never your friend in the first place.

Your number one priority is to be true to yourself. If you can't be true to yourself you can't be true to anything, and that means you can't be trusted. Well, it does, doesn't it?

So my advice, for what it's worth (if you're still asking), is to speak your mind, tell the truth, and watch the world around you change.

*

Many people have asked me about my personal history and about what I did before I started making videos, so here are a few biographical snapshots from memory. Feel free to skip this section and go straight to the transcripts if you like. I won't hold it against you.

One question I'm asked a lot is whether I'm Irish or British. The short answer is both. I was born in Ireland, but I grew up in south London and I carry a British passport. However, for many years I had an Irish passport which served me well until it expired and I had to get it renewed at the Irish embassy in London.

I needed to get the application signed by a professional person who had known me for two years, which, at that time, I didn't have, so I called the embassy and asked if I could go to a lawyer with proof of identity and get them to vouch for me.

"There's no need for that," came the reply. "Just get your priest to sign it."

"What priest?"

"Your local parish priest."

"I don't have a local parish priest."

"But everybody has a priest."

"I don't even know any priests."

"If you're Irish you must know a priest."

"Not me."

"Ah, you must."

This went on until it became clear that Father Dougal was going to take some shifting on the priest thing, so I decided to cut my losses and get a British passport, which meant becoming a British citizen, something I was more than happy to do.

Thankfully, at no stage of the process did I have to consult a priest. However, I did have to swear to defend the Queen.

As an atheist I could have done it with a simple affirmation, but instead I chose to swear on the Bible. That's right, I swore on the Holy Bible to defend the Queen. It's the kind of thing I had always wanted to do but never thought I'd get the opportunity, so when it came along I grabbed it with both hands. Now, if the Queen comes round my way and needs defending, I'll spring into action like a trained corgi. I won't need telling twice.

The best part was when the solicitor leaned across his desk, shook my hand, and said: "Welcome to Britain." I had to chuckle because I had probably lived here longer than he had, but I thanked him anyway for his good wishes and asked him to direct me to the nearest benefit office. That soon wiped the smile off his face.

I was raised as a Catholic (surprise surprise), meaning I was taken to church every week until I was old enough to put a stop to it. Though mildly fascinated by the pomp and ritual of the Catholic mass, the Latin chanting, the incense and so on, I couldn't take the beliefs seriously even as a child. I thought it was all nonsense, and I couldn't understand why adults behaved as if it was true.

My family moved around a lot and I went to several schools, including a grammar school and a comprehensive. I saw both sides of that argument and I hated them both. Consequently my education is lacking, and it's entirely my own fault. I was a frequent truant and I was frequently caned. What can I say? I'm not proud of it now.

I left school at sixteen and took the first job that came my way as a kitchen porter in the revolving restaurant on top of the Post Office Tower in central London. It revolved three times every hour, allowing diners to enjoy a panoramic view of a newly smog-free city spread out in all directions like a giant ashtray. It was quite the thing at the time.

The job was my first exposure to what might be called multiculturalism, as the kitchen was a polyglot environment where every chef seemed to be of a different nationality, with the frequent misunderstandings and temperamental rows to prove it. The food, however, was British to a fault.

We got five shillings an hour cash in hand, which meant that some of the porters and dishwashers were men who slept in the street and came up every day for alcohol money, so you never knew who you'd be working with from day to day, or what sort of mood they'd be in. The frequent arguments and tantrums got the better of me after a couple of months, and despite the notable perk of prime steak every day for lunch (I didn't become a vegetarian until a few years later) I finally quit and got a more respectable job as a shipping clerk in Fenchurch Street.

One day during a rare interview with the company chairman, Mr Powell-Brett (Powell pronounced "Pole"), he asked me what my father did for a living. I told him my father was an accountant, thinking it would impress him. In truth, my father wasn't quite an accountant; he worked as a settler for a turf accountant, or a bookie. He was also a compulsive gambler. Not the ideal combination. As a result we never had much money, although personally I never felt poor, and generally I had a happy childhood, even if the old man couldn't be trusted to bring home his wages every Friday.

Mr Powell-Brett looked me up and down with frank distaste. I was wearing a suit that looked as if it had been slept in, mainly because it had been slept in.

"That suit looks as if it has been slept in."

"No, sir, it's the fashion."

(I always called him sir. Everybody did. Except the office manager, Mr Birtwistle, who was allowed to call him PB.)

PB eyed me over his half-moon specs.

"How much are we paying you, boy?"

"Seven pounds ten shillings a week, sir."

"I'm going to increase it to seven pounds fifteen shillings a week, and I want you to take the extra five shillings and save up for a new suit."

Five shillings was the equivalent of twenty-five pence today, but it bought a lot more. You could treat yourself to a Wimpy (a British version of the hamburger – thin, dry and extremely unpleasant) and a milkshake, and still have enough left over for ten cigarettes and a pint of Double Diamond bitter. Needless to say that's where the extra money went. No new suit was ever purchased, nor was it ever likely to be.

I drifted in and out of various jobs (including parks gardener, builder's labourer, and a stint on the assembly line at Ford's in Southampton) and travelled a bit in Europe, mostly Spain, until 1971 when I met my wife to be, and a few months later we went to Israel, where we spent the summer of 1972 working on a kibbutz.

Before going to Israel I knew very little about the country and had no strong opinions about it. I knew about the Six Day War, of course, and I knew that the Arabs had been so busy crowing about their plans to wipe Israel off the map that they allowed the Israelis to bomb all their aircraft before they could get off the ground, so I admired the Israelis for their pluck, but really I just wanted to go somewhere warm.

At the time I was working in a second-hand furniture store in south London. It was something between a warehouse and a vast market stall; a labyrinth of wardrobes, sideboards, kitchen cabinets and drop-leaf tables stacked under corrugated plastic, but otherwise in the open air. Not much fun in winter. Definitely a scarf and gloves job.

One day my friend Richard told me about Israel and how you could work on a kibbutz as a volunteer, picking oranges and avocados in the morning and lying on a beach all after-noon. It could be arranged from an office in London, he told me. They assign you to a kibbutz; all you have to do is get there and move in.

I've always had a taste for uncomplicated processes, and on a miserable January afternoon in Forest Hill that sounded like the ticket for me.

When I told the boss I was leaving to go to Israel, he looked puzzled. "Are you Jewish?"

"No."

"Then why Israel?"

I wanted to say: "Because even a war zone is better than this Dickensian dump."

But I told him about the kibbutz, and he looked genuinely amazed.

"You're going to work for no money?"

He simply couldn't understand it. I could barely understand it myself, to be honest, but I went anyway.

We stayed on kibbutz Kabri in northern Galilee, a few miles from the border with Lebanon. The work was simple and satisfying and the accommodation basic (a small cinderblock hut with a couple of beds, a table, a chair and little else), but the food was fresh and plentiful and the people easy to get along with.

We rose each day at four and worked till lunchtime (except on Saturdays) and we soon got used to checking our boots for scorpions every morning and keeping an eye out for wild pigs in the fields.

My work was mostly picking avocados and pomegranates, neither of which I had ever seen, let alone tasted before. And later in the season when the rain came I harvested bananas, carrying the bunches through ankle-deep mud to the waiting truck.

At that time my politics were still left-wing, and I saw the kibbutz as the perfect socialist society. Each person gave what they could and took what they needed, and no money ever changed hands. Everyone seemed happy and contented, and there appeared to be a genuine community effort to keep things sweet. However, I realised even then that a kibbutz possesses an essential safety valve that a socialist state doesn't have: i.e. the people who don't want to live like that are free to move to the city, get a job, and make as much money as possible like everybody else, while the kibbutz, for its part, can sell its produce on the open market and also make as much money as possible.

While in Israel we took time out to visit Jerusalem and the West Bank, so I know what it's like to walk around an Arab town in the company of an attractive western woman (I don't recommend it).

My most abiding memory of the West Bank, apart from the leering, groping Arab men, is of the interior wall of a café in Nablus entirely covered by a picture of Nasser.

Back on the kibbutz we worked through the summer, enjoying the company, enjoying the place, getting to know several kibbutzniks well enough to be guests in their homes, and spending time on the beach at nearby Nahariya, or drinking beer and eating pastries in the cafés. Then one day in September we heard that eleven Israeli athletes had been murdered by Arab terrorists at the Munich Olympics, and everything changed. It was as if a dark cloud had descended on the country and chilled it to the marrow, and it seemed that everywhere you looked there was public grief. For a few sombre days afterwards we watched smoke from Israeli missiles rising to the north across the Lebanese border, then we decided it was time to move on.

The following year we got married and went to live in my wife's home town in Canada where I got a job pulling boards in a sawmill.

The interior of British Columbia was a whole new world for me. The people of Greenwood were wonderfully warm and welcoming, and I soon settled in.

I loved the wild country and the fresh air and water, the

distinct seasons and the crazy temperatures, and I was a little alarmed by the proximity of wildlife.

The town occupies a narrow valley, and occasionally black bears would come down the hill looking for food. A couple of times we found a bear in our yard; you just had to be careful. And one day shortly after I started at the sawmill we found a rattlesnake in a lumber pile that had everyone scattering until a carrier driver cheerfully beat it to death with a pike pole.

I worked at the sawmill in summer so hot it would melt tar and winter so cold your eyelashes would freeze, doing various jobs from swamping on the dry kilns to feeding the stripper stacker to loading boxcars. The money was good and we could afford to buy a house and a pickup truck. Over the next few years both our daughters were born, and things ticked along nicely for a while.

Canada is officially a multicultural country, but it would be more accurate to call it multi-ethnic, which is what it was when I lived there, and it was all the richer for it. I lived and worked alongside people from all kinds of backgrounds, and there were never any problems, because everybody wanted to fit in.

In particular there was a large Japanese community in Greenwood, people who had been rounded up and moved to the interior during the Second World War simply because they were Japanese. Many had had their property confiscated and they were generally treated in a very shabby way. However, they didn't develop a grievance culture and start rioting in the street like some we could mention. By the time I got there they were all happily integrated, and, while I was there, some of my best pals were Japanese Canadians.

I often relaxed after work in the bar with the local loggers and miners, and when one day I was offered the chance to go into the woods as a logger I didn't need asking twice.

I had no experience of logging, of course, and I soon realised it's the kind of job you pick up quickly if you want to stay alive. The main attraction for me, apart from the outdoor aspect, was the regular day shift. I didn't mind the work at the mill. It was simple and repetitive and it kept me physically fit, but I disliked waiting around all evening to go to work on the graveyard shift. I could never enjoy myself fully (meaning I couldn't drink beer). I wanted day shift, and logging provided it.

We got up at four every morning and drove seventy miles up a dirt track road, about ten of us crammed into a four-by-four crummy with almost everyone smoking. (This was back when cigarettes were only bad for you physically, not socially.) On arrival we piled out and a cloud of smoke billowed out with us as if sending a signal back to town that we had arrived at camp.

My first job was bucking the trees the skidders dragged in, trimming the limbs and topping and tailing them, turning them into respectable logs. I soon learned how to run a chainsaw and keep it sharp. I also ran skidder whenever there was a spare machine. I had been operating forklifts and other machines at the mill, so I soon picked it up.

We worked summer, fall and winter (you can always tell when an area has been logged in winter because the stumps are about six feet high), but we didn't work in spring because six feet of melting snow causes oceans of water to cascade down the mountains, and it's too dangerous.

Logging is tough enough anyway, and it seemed to me that

hardly a week went by that you didn't hear that Harry or Gus from a nearby town had broken his back when a tree fell on him. I didn't relish the thought of that happening to me, so I studied the problem and decided it was probably best to get out of the way when the tree is falling. This turned out to be a lot easier said than done, as I discovered when one of the fallers got hurt so badly he had to retire, and I got a chance to take his place.

Falling trees is the most dangerous job in a dangerous profession, so the money is better. I had to pester the boss to distraction before he agreed to give me a chance, but eventually he caved in and I went to work.

I wish I could say I was a roaring success, but the truth is I found it very hard. With a young family, I took chances I shouldn't have, and I very nearly killed myself more than once.

My lack of experience roared back at me each time I revved the saw, and I seemed to do something wrong whenever I dropped a tree. It would spin on the stump and fall the wrong way, or it would lean back and pinch the bar and I'd be desperately hammering wedges in to try and tip it the other way, or it would split into a "barber chair", a nasty surprise where the tree goes over, but splits from the bottom up, leaving a shard of wood a couple of yards high on the stump; as the tree pivots on this, the butt swings up like an uppercut, and if you happen to be standing there it can remove your head from your shoulders.

Falling trees taught me how to stay fully in the present moment and focus my attention on the here and now (something for which I'm still grateful). With snags and "widowmakers" everywhere there was no room for internal dialogue. Every action was too important to be automatic. Every step had to be actively considered. Slowly over the weeks and months I got the hang of it, my confidence rose, and I started to relax.

Then a tree fell on me.

It was my own stupid fault and I should have been killed.

I had tried to save time by undercutting several pine with the intention of dropping a large fir into them to knock them all down at once. Unfortunately, one of the smaller trees went part way over then came back on me. It happened so fast I had no chance to react. Luckily, I tripped and fell into a natural hollow, the tree fell across it, and I emerged from under it virtually without a scratch.

Praise the Lord?

Surely if I was ever going to turn to God it would be at a moment like that. Many a Christian would have been on their knees for the next half hour giving thanks and praise, but I can honestly say that God never crossed my mind as I crawled from under that tree – until I found my chainsaw crushed like a tin can, and I cursed him to the high heavens.

A little while later (when I had stopped shaking) I decided it might be prudent to look for an easier way to make a living.

By 1982 we were back in London, and I was looking for a creative angle. In those days a lot of people were calling themselves poets who clearly weren't, so I wrote some stuff and sent it to Michael Horovitz who included me in his annual wordfest, the Poetry Olympics at the Young Vic theatre, where I surprised myself by not feeling at all nervous in front of a full house.

I performed a piece called *Create that World*, a parody of the old TV game show *Name that Tune*, in which God claims that he can "create that world" in six days. It built to quite a climax and there were a few good laughs in it. It went down a storm at the Young Vic and the next day my picture was in *The Times* (you can see it on my website). Shortly afterwards *Time Out* magazine got in touch and asked me to write a weekly topical poem at ninety pounds a throw (ker-ching), which I did for about six months until the novelty wore off.

At the same time I began to get work on the grant-funded New Variety circuit where nobody was allowed to say the word "cunt" on stage (we were specifically warned) and whose audiences came mainly from the Socialist Workers Party and the self-consciously "right on" *Guardian*-reading middle-class left, from which there was usually a fair sprinkling of both men and women dressed in unisex dungarees.

They called it New Variety because every show was a mixed bag of ranting "poets", jugglers, musical acts, political theatre groups and various oddball street performers, and it was strictly non-sexist and non-racist (apart from being anti-men and anti-white people).

It was the beginning of what we now know as political correctness, and its audiences were the forerunners of the modern multicultural thought police, with exactly the same embarrassing double standards. Every remark from every performer was rigorously examined for ideological purity, yet you could see feminists from Women Against Violence Against Women drooling over a dreadlocked black poet as he explained how he wanted to beat up Mrs Thatcher. You get the idea.

One night I made a joke about how few famous women there are in history and I was accosted as I left the stage by an angry crop-haired bull dyke in Doc Martens who told me that there were plenty of women who should have been famous but they were ignored by men. This was precisely the point of the joke, but it was lost on her as she ploughed through the history lecture, jabbing at me with her finger and finishing with a stern: "Get it right."

It was late, the bar was closing and I couldn't be bothered to argue, so I told her to go and fuck herself, and the dungareed eunuchs in the immediate vicinity reacted as if I had snapped to attention and shouted "Heil Hitler". Apparently, I had committed the ultimate sin of exhibiting male aggression and had broken through some kind of fourth wall and fractured their world. Shortly after this I was banned from New Variety venues for a couple of years for punching a member of the audience. (Well, somebody had to.)

By the mid-eighties the Comedy Store had moved from its original strip-club setting to new premises in Leicester Square, and one night I went along to the midnight show to take a look. I was impressed. It was a seething bear pit awash with alcohol, and the atmosphere was electric.

How I got a gig at the Comedy Store I don't know, but I did. I must have done OK, because they booked me for six consecutive Saturdays and I never looked back. I worked there regularly for the next ten years or so, both in the main weekend shows and as a member of the weekly Tuesday topical team, the Cutting Edge, with whom I performed at the Edinburgh Fringe in 1991 as the Soviet Union was collapsing, and we dealt with the daily hangover by writing ourselves into a creative frenzy keeping up with events and radically updating the show each day.

Through the late eighties and early nineties the comedy circuit expanded steadily outside London to encompass the whole country, and I was working every night, often doing two or three gigs a night on weekends. I played scores of theatres, comedy clubs and universities all over Britain and got to know every major city and most of the towns.

On more than one occasion I performed four times in one night, opening the eight o'clock show at the Comedy Store, then up to Highbury Corner for a nine o'clock start at the T&C2 (my favourite gig, alas now defunct), then over to Shoreditch to close at the Comedy Cafe, and finally back to the Store for the midnight show, followed by a few beers and a three o'clock taxi ride home with a pocket full of cash. Salad days.

As a stand-up, I always had a political edge, and by the time the Rushdie affair exploded in 1989 I was well established on the circuit and turning over a lot of topical material. We didn't know it at the time, but we were getting our first taste of the reality of Islam's intolerant hysteria and its propensity to violence as a first resort, and also of the inherent spinelessness of the liberal left which abandoned Rushdie to his fate without a backward glance.

Khomeini's fatwa should have been stamped on at once, and free speech should have been nailed to the mast, but instead Rushdie was condemned by the "liberal intelligentsia", the very people he thought he could count on for support.

"It's wrong that he's been sentenced to death," they said, "but he brought it on himself by insulting one of the world's great religions."

I couldn't believe I was hearing it, and I was hearing it all the time.

Rushdie's betrayal by the chattering classes gave a green light to the bigots and bullies of Islam and set the tone for the campaign of baseless grievance-mongering and knee-jerk offence that has plagued western society for the last two decades. And, incredibly, nobody seems to have learned a thing. We see the same wretched attitude today from critics of Dutch politician Geert Wilders, a man who has to live with a twenty-four-hour armed guard for criticising the religion of permanent offence. As with Rushdie, you get the feeling that some of his "liberal" critics would actually like to see him killed, for the ultimate multiculti crime of damaging "community cohesion".

As soon as the Rushdie affair broke, jokes about the mullahs and their dopey religion became a regular feature of my stand-up set, and throughout the nineties I got a little tired of hearing journalists complain that comedians were afraid to criticise Islam, when I and several others were doing it every week at the Comedy Store.

It's true that nobody on radio or TV was doing it, because they weren't allowed to. They still aren't. When I started working for BBC radio in what was supposed to be a topical satire show it quickly became clear that jokes about religion would not be encouraged and jokes about Islam would not be tolerated. I blotted my copybook one day at a script meeting when the producer stopped me in mid-punchline and informed me solemnly that her father was a Muslim, to which I replied: "Great. Tell him the drinks are on me."

If the word "Islamophobic" can be used legitimately, it can be used to describe the BBC, which is genuinely terrified of Islam (the outgoing director general admitted as much in

February 2012). If not for this I might never have made a single video, and this book wouldn't exist.

My last appearance on BBC radio was butchered so badly in the edit I finally got the message. I realised the only way I would ever be able to say anything publicly critical of religion would be to write a stage show and hustle it around the circuit. So I wrote the show in three months, called it *Faith Hope & Sanity – A few jokes about religion before it kills us all*, and put it on at the tiny Etcetera Theatre in Camden Town.

Time Out's now legendary comedy critic Malcolm Hay did me a favour with a full-page interview which helped to sell out the theatre for the entire week and I actually made money, something almost unheard of in fringe theatre.

On the very first night I was approached after the show by an elderly gentleman who had been sitting at the back taking notes. He congratulated me on an excellent performance (it wasn't that great, to be honest) and introduced himself as the Messiah.

He told me that he intended to reveal himself to the world at the turn of the year, at which time he promised to ensure that my show was given worldwide television coverage for the benefit of mankind.

Wow! A Messiah on my very first night (and such a perceptive critic). I couldn't believe my luck. I thanked him for his good wishes, and off he went.

Well, you can imagine my disappointment when the new year came and went with no sign of the returning Messiah, and no worldwide television.

Ruefully, I dismissed the old man as a fraud, booked another week at the Etcetera, and went online to look for ways to publicise the show, while contemplating the less than attractive prospect of taking it on the road and building an audience that way.

Then one day I clicked on a link and, as if by a miracle, there was internet video, the poor man's worldwide television, staring me right in the face. (They say God works in mysterious ways.)

Could this be true? A public platform with no editors, house lawyers or committees to negotiate, no gatekeepers or censors to get past, no script approval needed? Just a camera (check) and a big mouth (check).

Since then I've made 118 videos, more than eleven hours of constant talking, not one word of which would have been approved for transmission by the BBC or any other broadcaster, yet to date they've been viewed, at a conservative estimate, more than seventy million times.

I hope you enjoy these transcripts, even if you don't agree with everything. They represent my honest immediate response to situations and events as they happened, and they've been transcribed verbatim, so the usual caveat applies that it might not all be perfect prose. You'll find extensive press links on the YouTube versions of the videos to back up what I say in each one.

Reading through them now, there are one or two places where I might have phrased things more temperately with more time to reflect, but that's the nature of the beast, and it goes without saying (but I'll say it anyway) that I stand by every word in this book, I don't apologise for a single comma, and I never will.

61

Aggressive Atheism

November 28, 2009

I've been hearing quite a lot of bleating and whining in the press lately about aggressive intolerant atheism, as if that's somehow a bad thing. It seems religion can dish it out OK, but it can't take it, like a street thug who calls the police when his victims fight back.

Aggressive atheism is really defensive atheism, because right now nothing is more aggressive than political religion. Being an atheist or a secularist today is no longer a matter of opting out, but of actively fending off, so I'd say that any abuse religion gets, it's got coming ten times over.

Besides, I don't think it's possible to be too aggressive in defending freedom of speech, which is, of course, absolutely sacred, as we all know; much, much more sacred than any god or prophet or scripture could or will ever be from now until the end of time, or for eternity, whichever lasts longer.

People sometimes tell me: "You're just as intolerant as the people you criticise."

Really? I hope so, because somebody has to be.

There are some things I'm very intolerant of, and there's no point in trying to deny that. Let's see now, there's misogyny and sexism. I'm extremely intolerant of them. I hope that doesn't offend.

Racism? Anti-Semitism? No, no tolerance there at all, I'm afraid. Sorry about that. Homophobia, perhaps? Not a shred of tolerance to be found. Gosh, I do have some issues, don't I?

How about cruelty to animals? Again, absolutely no tolerance whatsoever.

But brace yourselves, because that's not the half of it. Not only am I openly and brazenly intolerant of all those things, but if religion is used as an excuse for any of them, I'm afraid I become aggressively hostile. And what's more, I don't apologise for that because I have no need to apologise for it, and neither do you.

I'm always being told I should respect people's feelings. OK, but what about my feelings? What about the feeling of utter revulsion I get whenever I think of the god of the desert and the horrible thoughts and deeds he inspires? This god is my Satan. When I hear his name I smell sulphur. When I hear his words I smell death. I can see that his filthy religion has polluted the world I have to live in far more thoroughly than any fossil fuel could ever dream of.

And I can see that everything about this god has been purposely designed to poison our experience of life on earth, not to enhance it; to keep us fearful, to suppress knowledge, to curtail freedom and creativity, and to celebrate death. It's nothing less than the sanctified dumbing down of the human race, and demanding respect for it is frankly an insult that deserves to be repaid with considerable interest.

Religion deserves no respect at all, because a) it offers no respect at all, and b) it offers no evidence at all. Evidence is actually unwelcome as it removes the need for faith, and that would be such a waste of all that phoney virtue.

Faith is one of three phoney virtues, the others being piety and righteousness. Not so much a trinity as three ugly sisters. Unlike the witches in Macbeth who see the world in a cauldron, these three have done their best to turn the place into one (praise the Lord) and they're still going strong.

Among the many gifts from these delightful muses we have the Middle East conflict for a start, and that's the gift that just seems to keep on giving. Not to mention the cancer at the heart of it, Jerusalem, that jewel in the desert, that celestial piss-hole in the sand, from which the spiritual Black Death of the Middle-Eastern desert has oozed and spread throughout this world like a vile oil slick, coating and contaminating everything it touches with the thick slime of pious ignorance – only we don't call it ignorance, we call it faith.

What a horrible little word that is – faith, exuding its fake aura of purity and virtue, while fronting some of the ugliest ideas this planet has ever seen; closing people's hearts when it should be opening them; making them proud of things they should be ashamed of, and ashamed of things they should be proud of.

When we look at the violent barbarism of the Islamic world we can see that no righteous act is too depraved for a mind that claims the full licence allowed by faith. If you take this god

35

completely at his word you can be just like him, a vicious, heart-less monster, and feel good about it.

Even in the civilised world, nothing is too dishonourable to be sanitised by faith. It was faith, remember, that deprived gay people in California of their basic civil rights on the same day that America elected a black president. It was faith that persuaded Christian black people to send the gays to the back of the bus.

All this would be ugly enough on its own, but because of the free pass that we consistently give to this fake virtue of faith, religion is now completely out of control. It's already got its hands around the throat of the United Nations, and it's pushing for a worldwide blasphemy law to protect people from hearing words that might crowbar their tiny minds out of the Stone Age.

The very concept of blasphemy is a perfect illustration of the cowardly immaturity of the religious mind and the empti-ness of religion itself. If religion contained any truth it could be ridiculed, insulted or even defiled without being diminished in any way. Its truth would shine through undimmed, unblem-ished, shaming those who abused it into silence.

But that's not how things are. Religion is prickly, intolerant and ultra-defensive precisely because it's brittle and fragile. It's about as substantial as a meringue. It's all front and no sub-stance. It's had thousands of years to make its case, and all it has produced is sophistry and violence and a raft of morals that would shame a rattlesnake.

And no amount of windbaggery and flimflam from clergy can any longer disguise the simple bald fact that there is noth-ing there. The only true thing about religion is that it's false. Its claim to higher knowledge is laughable. It doesn't even have any lower knowledge. Not one of its ludicrous claims about reality would have a hope in hell of standing up in a court of law, and it's time we stopped treating them as if they do.

That's all we're saying, and that's all we're asking, and anyone who thinks that's too aggressive knows what they can do with themselves, and if they don't I'll be more than happy to tell them.

62

Thank God for Andy Choudary

January 14, 2010

Whenever we think that Islam's reputation couldn't possibly be dragged any lower, we know we can always rely on Anjem Choudary to pop up like some ludicrous bearded pig on a stick, bristling with so much fake righteous indignation you could warm your hands on it. He's irrepressible, isn't he? Like hospital food, you just can't keep him down.

You may remember him as the former cider-guzzling dope-smoking porn-ogling Andy Choudary of yesteryear. Well, he has come a long way since those days and now he's one of Britain's best-known benefit scroungers.

He calls himself a sharia judge, which would be true if the word "sharia" meant "imaginary". In fact, he isn't qualified to judge a knobbly knees competition.

Many people in Britain consider him something of a mystery man, in that it's a mystery why he's not in prison for treason. An even greater mystery is why we're obliged to subsidise his noxious public ravings.

Although he claims to speak from a moral standpoint, his actions show he has the morality of a tick, claiming, as he does, £25,000 a year from the state he despises so much – that's from you and me and all the pensioners who helped build this country and who now live on subsistence level while Andy Choudary is free to live a life of leisure, stirring up hatred (lots and lots of hatred), insulting the living and the dead, praising terrorists and calling for gay people to be executed, among other choice comments.

Some of his remarks have a cartoon-like quality, as when he called recently for Buckingham Palace to be turned into a mosque. I agree Buckingham Palace could be put to better use, but so could every mosque. I'd like to see them all turned into pubs – for the sake of community cohesion, of course, and we all know how important that is. (I'd be much more inclined to enter a mosque to find out what it's all about if I knew it served a good real ale.)

His latest stunt, which had everybody in Britain very animated over the last week or so, was a proposed protest march which seemed specifically calculated to insult the relatives of British soldiers who have died in battle. And this proved a step too far for the government who have decided to ban his entire organisation starting from today, which I think is a stupid move (nothing unusual for this government) and a threat to freedom of speech (again nothing unusual for this government.)

Andy Choudary would be a nobody (well, he is a nobody, but he'd be an unheard-of nobody) if the tabloid press hadn't puffed him up and turned him into the laughing stock he is. And yes, it's been great fun for the rest of us up to a point, but we shouldn't forget that there are more subtle minds than his at work in the same cause: people who talk in diplomatic terms publicly about dialogue and respect because they know that's where the government money is. But they want the same thing he does; they want an Islamic state in Britain, only he's stupid enough to shout about it all the time.

The *taqiyya* merchants at the Muslim Council of Britain must tear their hair out in frustration every time they see this buffoon in the media, because they know he does more than anyone to alert people to the true nature of their backward, intolerant and deeply unpleasant religion.

People say Choudary doesn't represent Muslims, and that's undoubtedly true. I know many Muslims think he's completely insane, and who could argue with that? But he does represent Islam, in that he represents the aggressive Islam that has become such a huge problem in the free world, the so-called pure Islam that Saudi money is busy pushing into western society with the connivance of the dhimmis-in-waiting in the multicultural appeasement lobby; the Islam that seeks to attack the fundamental values that make us what we are, knowing that if they can be cracked everything else will fall apart. Like the principle of freedom of speech, which is under repeated attack at the Third World pressure group we call the United Nations. Or the principle that was established in this country eight hundred years ago in the Magna Carta that everyone is entitled to swift and fair justice and nobody is above the law. Well, that was before Islam came along.

We discovered last summer that there are eighty-five sharia courts operating quietly in Britain that the government had no intention of telling us about, and they're all entitled to discriminate quite openly against women in a way that would be illegal for anybody else. Would we tolerate an institution where people of a certain colour were treated that way, where their word was worth half that of somebody of another colour? Not a chance. So why the double standards when it comes to women? Why do we collude with the poisonous idea that women are somehow inferior and incapable of self-determination? Because that is what we're doing in twenty-first century Britain thanks to Islam, and thanks to the Labour Party; women's fundamental rights are worth less than the seventh-century prejudices and superstitions of ignorant men.

But if you really want an example of how political correctness has made us less civilised, then look no further than the obscenity of religious slaughter that has crept into our society like a disease thanks to Islam, and thanks to the Labour Party, where millions of animals are now killed in needless pain and distress, in violation of every law on animal cruelty, for the sake of human superstition. That's beyond disgraceful. It's beyond disgusting. It's a sin, if that word means anything at all.

The opinion polls are telling us now that there's grave disquiet in Britain about Islam, and if things don't change it's only going to get worse. Banning the likes of Andy Choudary is merely cosmetic. It's designed to distract people's attention from the Labour Party's deliberate Islamisation of our society. It won't make anybody safer. All it will do is give extremists a legitimate grievance about double standards, and threaten everybody else's freedom of speech.

Admittedly, poor old Andy Choudary will now have to go to the trouble of thinking up a whole new name for his organisation, which could take him anything up to two seconds, so he has been well and truly put in his place, hasn't he?

In the meantime, in New Labour's new Islamic Britain it will be business as usual. More uncontrolled immigration, more Muslim ghettos, more extremist mosques, more hate-preaching imams, more sharia courts, more prayer rooms at work (they're fun, aren't they?), more state-supported faith schools where little girls are forced to dress like nuns, more halal meat creeping into your kids' school meals without you being told about it, more restrictions on eating lunch at your desk during Ramadan in case somebody chooses to be offended, more Muslim-only swimming days for those delicate souls who just can't bear to mix with the kuffar, more state benefits for extra wives, more forced marriages the authorities do nothing about out of cultural sensitivity, more female genital mutilation ignored by the police for the same cowardly reason, more universities encouraging extremism on campus and not being held to account, more frivolous lawsuits exploiting human rights legislation at the behest of the ever-growing "feelings" industry, and lots more public money for divisive Islamist pressure groups who speak for nobody but themselves. All accompanied, of course, by the steady relentless erosion of our basic freedom of expression for the sake of our old friend "community cohesion".

That's what we've got in store because that's what's gone before. And if things don't change, you know it's only a matter of time before you and your family are woken up every morning at five o'clock by some self-indulgent lunatic shouting across the rooftops.

Andy Choudary is the pilot fish for that society. He's the bell-wether. He's showing us the shape of things to come in all its stark insanity if we don't change direction. He's showing us what the Islamists at the Muslim Council of Britain have in store for Britain if they ever get their way. And in that he's actually doing us a huge favour, only he's too thick to realise it, thank goodness.

So thank you, Andy, for all your help. It's really very much appreciated. Please don't let this little setback put you off (I know you won't). Hurry up and re-form your scruffy little gang of hysterical fuzzy-faced nutjobs under a new name and get that ugly mug of yours back in the media where it belongs, because goddammit, you crazy bastard, we need you.

63

The Crooked Judges of Amsterdam

February 5, 2010

This week in an Amsterdam courtroom we saw the beginning of what could be both the trial of the century and the crime of the century. What an honour for the Netherlands so early in the century.

In the most determined statement of dhimmitude we've yet seen in Europe (and that's saying something), the Dutch authorities are pushing ahead with the prosecution of an elected parliamentarian for the crime of embarrassing them with the truth.

There's an ideological fervour about this prosecution that's almost religious in its intensity, because, let's be clear, this is a heresy trial by any other name. They can't refute Mr Wilders' statements, so instead they've resorted to the kind of cheap legal stunt we'd expect from the likes of Mugabe to shut their opponent up.

They've accused him of being divisive and inflammatory. And yes, sometimes the truth can be divisive and inflammatory if it's been suppressed for long enough and has become sufficiently taboo, as it clearly has in the Netherlands, because according to the prosecution it doesn't even matter that what he says is true. What matters is that it's illegal. Well, when the truth is against the law there's something seriously wrong with the law, because when the truth is no defence there is no defence, and the law has no anchor, so it will drift where the wind of political expedience blows. And this week it blew straight into a crooked courtroom in Amsterdam where justice will now be forced to fight for its life, starved of the oxygen of truth that gives it life.

These are desperate tactics from desperate people who have tied themselves up in such knots of relativist guilt they're incapable of acknowledging the truth, let alone dealing with it. They're like somebody who's prepared to chop off their own hand to avoid being seen scratching their arse in public.

What makes it worse is they're clinging to something that doesn't even exist. The multicultural bubble burst a long time ago, when Pim Fortuyn was murdered, when Theo van Gogh was murdered, both for the crime of expressing an opinion in what's supposed to be one of the world's leading liberal democracies. It was then the Dutch people and everybody else in Europe came face to face with multiculturalism, what it really is and what it really means.

On the surface it sounds like a pleasant word, evoking a kind of rainbow society of mutually enriching cultural perspectives, and what could be better than that? But that's not what it is at all, and that was never the intention.

If they had been honest from the start about what it really

is, Islamisation, they know they'd never have been allowed to get away with it. But people are beginning to realise now that Islam is in fact what they're getting, and it's all they're getting. And that's why the Freedom Party is leading the opinion polls in the Netherlands from nowhere in just a few short years. It's also why the ruling class is so desperate to destroy Mr Wilders before the next election, because they know his views are popular enough to change things, to put an end to the multicultural lie and give the Dutch people back their country. And that's why he's facing trial. Can I say that?

Maybe we shouldn't be too surprised it has come to this. After all, they do have a history of ganging up on their popular politicians in the Netherlands. Isn't that how Pim Fortuyn was murdered? Some leftist lunatic took the establishment and the press at their word that he was a public menace for opposing Islamisation, and killed him for it. Next day all the people who had been vilifying him were suddenly his best friends. They were shocked. How could this have happened? But they all know how it happened. The whole world knows how it happened. If it hadn't happened this trial wouldn't be taking place today, because Islam wouldn't be the problem it is today. And maybe Amsterdam would still be one of the world's favourite cities, and not the kind of place where gay people are afraid to go out for fear of being beaten up by gangs of Muslims youths.

The Dutch ruling class has shown that it's prepared to stoop to anything, even as far as undermining the very cornerstone of western civilisation, freedom of speech, to prop up a rotten ideology that's not only dead but whose corpse is now beginning to smell. And you know that smell. It's that pungent mix of authoritarianism and cowardice that we've become depressingly familiar with.

Certainly here in Britain we know all about it. We've had twelve years of it. And we haven't forgotten the shameful events of this time last year, when Mr Wilders was refused entry to Britain because our government allowed itself to be bullied and threatened by a handful of Muslim loudmouths who took it upon themselves to suppress free speech in a free country and were allowed to get away with it, because otherwise they might have been offended. Oh, perish the thought. Why the hell shouldn't Muslims be offended? What are they anyway, babies? Nobody gives a damn how offended the rest of us are at having our culture squatted by an aggressive religious totalitarianism and being told to shut up about it.

And that's why this trial is not just about the Netherlands. It affects all of us. The Dutch people have a well-deserved reputation for tolerance and open-mindedness – the very qualities, many would argue, that got them into this mess in the first place. So they're a bit further down the road of multicultural dhimmitude than most countries, but it's a road we're all travelling in the West. And, if we stay on it, we'll all arrive at the same unhappy crossroads in another courtroom in another country. It's only a matter of time.*

Fear of free speech is the symptom of a profoundly neurotic and dishonest society, which is what we've got on our hands now.

---

* In November 2010 Elisabeth Sabaditsch-Wolff went on trial in Austria for "denigrating religious teachings" by quoting violent passages from the Koran. In January 2011 Lars Hedegaard was prosecuted in Denmark for drawing attention to the comparatively high level of family rape in Islamic culture. The western press ignored both trials.

All over the western world it's the same sorry story. We have governments and police forces who cringe before Islam, while whittling away our civil liberties because of Islam. We have media that can't even use the word "Islam" in connection with terrorism, when the two things couldn't be more intimately connected if they were Siamese twins. Yet they're quite happy to label Mr Wilders as a far-right politician, in the kind of casual slander that passes for journalism these days, especially at the wretched BBC, who have been too politically correct even to acknowledge that this trial is taking place.

Anyone who isn't angry and ashamed that it is taking place doesn't deserve to live in a free society.

The trial has already left as dark a stain on Dutch history as McCarthyism left on American history, and it's only going to get worse, because not only have the crooked judges denied Mr Wilders the witnesses he needs to defend himself, but they've also made sure the trial will coincide with the election campaign, making it as difficult as possible for him to put his case to the people.

This man is a hero, not a criminal. And it's time the rest of us stood up and said so loud and clear, because there's too much at stake to be polite any more, and there's too much at stake to be afraid any more.

This intellectual terrorism has got to stop. Our birthright is being deliberately sold from under us by people who don't have the right of ownership. And we are now on the verge of bequeathing our children and grandchildren the kind of society that we wouldn't want to be born into. It doesn't get any more immoral or cowardly than that.

You know, in the English language we have an expression: Dutch courage. It's not really courage at all. It's the kind of courage you get when you've consumed too much alcohol. Well, now there's a new expression: Dutch justice. It's not really justice at all. It's the kind of justice you get when you've overdosed on cultural relativism and your spine has completely disappeared.

Shame on the Netherlands. Shame on the western media for not raising a howl of protest against this outrageous attack on our basic freedom. And shame upon shame on the crooked judges of Amsterdam.

64

Is Satan a Catholic?

March 27, 2010

Well, the Catholic Church continues to wash its dirty laundry in public, but they just can't seem to get those semen stains out, can they?

Now the Pope is in the spotlight for his own role as the architect of the cover-up, and therefore as facilitator of countless additional child rapes that could have been prevented if he and his Church hadn't been solely concerned about their own reputation – a reputation that now couldn't be any lower if Satan himself were to step onto the balcony in St Peter's Square to conduct Easter Mass with a choirboy on the end of his penis.

I've often thought that if Satan were a Christian he'd be a Catholic, so it came as no surprise to be told last week that Satan is, in fact, ensconced in the Catholic Church, and is working directly out of the Vatican, controlling operations from a big old captain's chair. OK, I made that last bit up, but only because it's the image that always comes to mind whenever I think of the Catholic Church.

And the Church's chief exorcist (yes, such a post really does exist – I don't know if it's higher or lower than, say, a wizard, but it's pretty high up in the mumbo-jumbo department) says that Satan is living in the Vatican. Well, I don't think much of his choice of company, but if Satan really is a Catholic it might help to explain some of the events of the last two thousand years.

Before the Reformation five hundred years ago all Christians in Europe were Catholics until the Church became too corrupt and debauched even for Christianity to stomach. But it is the original church of Christ, who said: "Upon this rock I will build my church," referring, of course, to St Peter (whose nickname, apparently, was Rock).

Unfortunately, human nature being what it is, the moment the Church was established it became a political organisation, which meant the consolidation of power and influence quickly became much more important than the message. (Message? What message? Oh, that message, of course.)

Inevitably this led to bickering about status and who got to wear the big ring and the fancy hat (you know, the really important stuff) until, before long, rival popes were facing each other with massed armies on the battlefield – in the name of Christ, naturally.

Even at this point, if Jesus had come back he would have said: "What are you people doing? I haven't been gone five minutes and already you're hacking each other to pieces like a bunch of savages. You've missed the point so completely, you're so far wide of the mark, it's beyond embarrassing. I feel as if I'm talking to chimpanzees," he'd say. (No offence, by the way, to any chimps who may be watching.)

And these are early days, don't forget. Jesus wouldn't yet know anything about all the other horrors that were about to be enacted in his name in the coming years; the Crusades, the Inquisition. He wouldn't know about the systematic suppression of knowledge and free thought that would characterise his Church for the next two thousand years. He wouldn't know about the conquest of the New World where the sacred cross of Jesus slashed and burned its way through entire populations in a way that modern jihadis can only dream about, imposing itself with unparalleled cruelty on civilisations half a world away that even today still don't quite know what hit them.

This is a Church that claims credit for keeping civilisation alive during the Dark Ages, but the truth is clergy were the only people who knew how to read and write and they made damn sure it stayed that way for hundreds of years. When the printing press was finally invented in Europe (seven hundred years after the Chinese invented it) the Church condemned it as a work of the Devil. (Takes one to know one, I guess.) The first man to translate the Bible into English was burned at the stake for his trouble, along with any astronomers and freethinkers they could round up when they weren't too busy making money from selling places in heaven, or rolling boulders of dogma into the path of science at every opportunity, from Galileo right through the Enlightenment (which might as well not have happened) up to the present day.

This is a church that condemned the smallpox vaccine, for Christ's sake, as a violation of God's will. It opposed anaesthesia in childbirth because a woman is supposed to suffer pain as punishment for Eve's sin. Not Adam's, Eve's sin – the sin of being a woman. It's one of the two main sins of the Christian faith, the other one being… anybody? That's right, the Jews killing Jesus. Which might explain why the minds of the righteous are so often filled with wicked women and evil Jews.

If the Jews really did kill Jesus they didn't do a very good job, because apparently he's still alive. Where's Mossad when you need them?

If Jesus ever comes back Mossad might as well bump him off because the Jews have already taken the blame for killing him. They might as well get the value. About seventy years ago they took the blame six million times as a direct result of the Catholic Church's rabid anti-Semitic teachings.

Europe is often referred to as a Judeo-Christian culture, but historically it's always been more of a Jew-hating Christian culture, thanks entirely to the Catholic Church. For centuries the Church in Europe preached open hatred against Jews, assiduously embedding Jew hatred into the very fabric of society, just as it is in many Muslim countries today. They made it virtuous to despise Jews, and it became, as it's becoming again in modern Europe, politically correct to be anti-Semitic.

And this was no lapse of judgment or flash of insanity by some crazy pope. This was centuries of institutionalised and deliberately focused hatred. When popes still had executive power, one after another they passed laws to victimise and humiliate Jews and steal their property. Jews weren't allowed to hold public office or to mix on equal terms with Christians. They were even obliged to wear yellow hats and scarves in some cases to identify themselves (ring any bells?). They were restricted to certain occupations and locations, and thanks to the blood libel (recently resurrected so tastefully by the Swedish press) they were massacred on a regular basis by the faithful, pious and righteous Christians with the Church's approval.

So, when Hitler came along, it was easy for him to pick on Jews because the Catholic Church had already made them such an easy target by consistently fingering them as hated Christ-killers. Hitler knew he'd have a lot of support because he knew that generations of Catholic children had been taught by their religion to hate Jews, just as many Muslim children are today. How could they not be influenced? How could society not be poisoned?

And Hitler, by the way, was a Catholic, not an atheist as people often claim. He was baptised a Catholic, and he was never excommunicated for his crimes. No Nazis were ever excommunicated by the Catholic Church, although every Communist on the planet was. Indeed, the Catholic Church actually provided documentation to help many Nazis escape to South America, or to certain Arab countries who wanted to exploit their expertise in exterminating Jews.

If you believe in Satan, and if you believe that Satan is responsible for all the evil in this world, then the Catholic Church is surely his most fiendishly brilliant creation, because when you look at its record it's hard to imagine how the Catholic Church could have had a more negative effect on human history than it has, and even harder not to conclude that any other organisation with its track record would be legislated out of existence as an enemy of humanity.

If the Catholic Church hadn't so consistently and virulently condemned the Jews for killing Jesus there would have been no

Holocaust. There would have been no reason for anyone to think about picking on Jews. And that means today there might be no Jewish state and no Middle East conflict. That's quite a lot to have on your conscience, isn't it? How fortunate for the Catholic Church that it doesn't possess a conscience. But at least it gives ordinary Catholics the opportunity to feel guilty about something real for a change, if they feel so inclined, and to reflect on the reality that the Jews didn't kill Jesus at all. The Catholic Church killed Jesus, and has spent the last two thousand years dragging his entrails through the dirt. And if he came back tomorrow he'd be the first to say so. You know it's true. We all do.

65

What I Know about Islam

April 18, 2010

One of the most common things people say to me is: "You know nothing about Islam." And it's true that I don't know very much about Islam, but it's also true that I know a lot more than I want to know, ever since Islam has been allowed to elbow its way into western society and thrust itself into everybody's face.

I know, for example, that Islam allows a man to beat his wife, and all over the internet I can find videos of Islamic "scholars" explaining exactly how to do this. These are the same "scholars" whose reading of Islam has turned the country of Saudi Arabia into the kind of place where a person can be executed for witchcraft, or where a father is allowed to sell his pre-pubescent daughter to a child rapist and still call himself a man.

I know that Islam encourages violence against apostates, against Jews and against homosexuals. And I know that anyone who dares to criticise it for this naked barbarism will be physically threatened and put in fear of their life.

I know that in the western world, rape is a crime against women by men, whereas in the Islamic world it's a crime by women punishable by guess who. Men.

And I know that for these reasons no other religion makes me feel quite as ashamed to be a human being as Islam does, and coming from a Catholic background, believe me, that is saying something.

I also know that the oil that generates the wealth to pay for the ongoing Islamisation of the West would still be in the ground if the wife-beating child-raping "scholars" of Islam had their way, because the internal combustion engine would never have been invented.

I know these things about Islam because everybody knows them.

But people keep telling me: "You are ignorant. You should read the Koran."

Well, OK, so I read the Koran. But then somebody said: "You read it in English? No, you have to read it in Arabic to truly understand it."

Ah, Arabic, eh? Well, OK, maybe I could learn Arabic. It would certainly be more than most of the Muslims on this planet have bothered to do. Let's see now, what else would Arabic be really useful for, apart from reading the Koran . . .?

I'll get back to you if I think of anything, but don't hold your breath, because it's precisely because of the influence of conservative Islamic "scholars" that the Arab world has become such a cultural backwater and the number of books translated into Arabic each year could probably fit into a briefcase, and still leave room for a thermos and sandwiches.

So anyway, I was reading the Koran in English like an igno-ramus, clumping through it in metaphorical hobnailed boots, so to speak. But one passage did catch my eye, and that was Surah 109; *al-Kafiroon* it's called, or "The Non-believers". And this verse says: I don't believe what you believe and you don't believe what I believe. You have your religion and I have mine.

And I thought: that sounds very reasonable, very tolerant, almost, dare I say it, like a religion of peace.

And then I got to thinking that if every person on the planet were to become a Muslim in the way the "scholars" and the professional whiners of Islam are always insisting, there would no longer be any need for that verse in the Koran. It would be effectively redundant, rendering the book imperfect, which is of course impossible because it's the pure word of God.

So clearly God in his infinite wisdom anticipated that not everybody would want to be a Muslim, or would be suited to being a Muslim for one reason or another, and he approved of that situation. Otherwise he wouldn't have said so in the book.

Although a number of people have kindly offered to answer any questions I may have about the Koran, I can't help but wonder why I should have any questions if it's the pure word of God. Is God not capable of expressing himself clearly and directly to me without ambiguity, even in a crass and unsubtle language like English? Surely, even to suggest such a thing is deeply blasphemous.

To explain or to interpret the Koran is surely an attempt to undermine the pure word of God, to adulterate it with a human perspective, and in the case of the "scholars" who depend for their very existence on such adulteration, with their own personal neuroses. Sealed, as they are, in their ignorant bubble of righteousness with nothing for company but chronic sexual repression and a pathological fear of women, the holy men of Islam have no knowledge and no wisdom and not a spiritual bone between them, so they have to rely instead on the only thing they do have – the capacity to generate fear, which is, of course, the lowest emotion a human being can have. Is that really the purpose of Islam?

The threat of crude violence is always the first option with these sad little men, because it's literally all they've got at their disposal. How empty is that? That's why apostates are killed in Islam, because the primitive throwbacks who define the religion simply don't know any other way. It's the "scholars" who call for the brutal punishments, who sanction the mutilations and executions, the monstrous treatment of women, the abuse of children, the murderous hatred towards Jews and homosexuals, and who have turned Islam from something that could have been beautiful into a dark inhuman religion of death, tainting all Muslims in the process; because if you're a Muslim these people have coloured the way the world sees you, and they're not doing you any favours. And that's one thing I do know, and so do you. If every Muslim was encouraged to read the Koran by listening to God through their own heart and not through somebody else's twisted mind, what a different and vibrant religion it might be.

66

Vote Small, Think Big

April 24, 2010

This is going to be a video about politics, not religion, because here in Britain we have an election coming up where we get a chance to vote for a new government. Isn't that exciting?

In a democracy, of course, you always get a choice. Do you want to be governed by the red or by the blue? It's entirely up to you. Do you want to be patronised or condescended to, by liars or by crooks? You get to choose. Would you prefer your fundamental values to be insulted or ignored, by conmen or by charlatans? In short, do you want your influence to be zero or nil, and when you would like to be listened to – never, or not at all? It's your choice.

Do you want some more choice? Take it or leave it. Now there's a real choice.

Some people say we should have proportional representation in Britain. I'd be happy with any kind of representation, wouldn't you?

I would like to see a new government, and part of me doesn't really give a damn who's in it as long as it doesn't include anybody from the Labour Party, an organisation that has shown itself to be without shame or principle, both spineless and authoritarian, both cowardly and warmongering at the same time.

Personally, I'll be voting for the UK Independence Party because I want to see the laws of this country made in this country by people who live here and who are accountable, and I don't think that's too much to ask.

Whoever you decide to vote for, you should know that this is the most important election we've ever had in Britain because this is the last chance we ever will have to reclaim our power of self-determination from the criminals who have stolen it.

So much of our autonomy has been handed to the European Union (where seventy-five percent of our laws now come from) that at this rate come the next election in five years' time our government will no longer be a government worth the name and this country will have ceased to exist as an independent nation.

And if you vote Conservative or Liberal Democrat or Labour in this election (and God help you if you vote Labour) you'll be helping to bring this about, and you'll be helping to put an end to democracy in the United Kingdom. Is that really what you want? Because all three parties are absolutely committed to seamless integration into the coming European superstate, and none of them intend to give the British people any say in the matter at all. Whatever that is, it's not democracy.

Time and again in Europe we've seen that the people's voice, the only voice that should count in a democracy, is the only voice that doesn't count, as every popular vote that's inconvenient to the ruling class is either ignored or overturned, because votes are merely window dressing to the European Union, which was purposely designed from the outset to be undemocratic, as a kind of bourgeois model of the old Soviet Union where everything is regulated and no decision-makers are accountable to anyone.

It's ruled by a council of appointed commissioners who can do what they like and who can't be removed by popular vote, because actual democracy is just too unpredictable. People have shown they can't be trusted to vote the right way, and that's why the European people are being eased out of the governing process and led nose-first into a federal dictatorship by a self-serving political class who have become a law unto themselves.

In Britain they've shown themselves time and again, not just with the European Union, but with other major issues like the war in Iraq, the multicultural nightmare, the banking bailouts. These history-shaping events were never subject to any kind of popular vote, and everyone knows that if they had been, none of them would have happened.

Everyone also knows that the MPs in all three parties are nothing but lobby fodder who vote exactly the way they're told because their whole poxy career depends on it. Why do you want someone like that to represent you? You're better than that, and you deserve better. We all do.

The truth is you don't have to vote for any of these people, and don't let the media brainwash you into thinking you do just because they're the only ones they ever talk about. Wherever you stand in the political spectrum, whether it's left or right or green or in between, you'll find a small party or an independent candidate who actually believes in what they're standing for and who will match your own views as well as any of these political corporations.

Of course, they'll try to persuade you that a vote for a small party is a wasted vote, that your vote won't count. Yet when you consider that the leaders of the Conservative and Labour parties are both proven barefaced liars, why would you want your vote to count for somebody like that, somebody you know is going to break every manifesto pledge and every cast-iron guarantee, because they've done it before? If either of them wins democracy will lose, and you know that too. Now that's what I call a wasted vote.

Maybe you're a lifelong Conservative or Labour voter and you don't really want to vote for the bastards again because you're as nauseated as anyone by all the blatant trough-snuffling and endless mealy-mouthed double talk, but you just can't shake off your tribalist instincts and you don't feel you have a choice.

Well, I'm here to tell you that you do have a choice. You have a real choice, and a real responsibility, and your vote will count. If it takes a hundred arrows to bring down an elephant, they're all necessary and they all count. And if we want to keep our freedom in this country (and I'm assuming that we do) we have to get people into Parliament who will vote the way their constituents want them to, and not the way they're told.

And it has to start from somewhere. As Gandhi said, you've got to be the difference you want to see in the world. There's no point waiting for somebody else to do it. It starts with you, and with me.

And if enough of us take the personal responsibility and actually do it, we can fracture this hardpan of complacent arrogance that's suffocating our democracy, and take back control of our own destiny.

And it starts with you. You have the power as an individual to withdraw your support and stop feeding this monster. You have the power to shoot your arrow into the charging beast. And it will count. But it's a power that you have to use, otherwise you will lose it, because in this election a vote for any of the three main parties is far more than just a wasted vote. It's a wasted opportunity that will likely never come again.

So just for this polling day, just this once, please do yourself and everyone else a favour. Vote for your own freedom. Vote small and think big.

67

Hello Angry Atheists

May 3, 2010

I've had a very hostile response to my last video from people who think my political views represent a betrayal of atheism, or of science, or of ordinary civilised values.

In fact I can't remember having quite as many metaphorical fingers poking my chest as I've had for the last week, but it hasn't been an altogether unpleasant experience. It's really quite amazing what you can learn about yourself from other people's perceptions. Here I was thinking I'm a liberal-minded freedom-loving democrat at heart, when in fact what I really am is a monstrous hypocritical right-wing reactionary xenophobic jingoistic flag-waving little Englander, a bigoted throwback who is scientifically illiterate and morally reprehensible. And not only that, I ought to be thoroughly ashamed of myself, and frankly I'm an embarrassment to anybody with a brain or any kind of decent human values. That's quite a lot of responsibility, isn't it? I only hope I can do you all justice and live up to it.

Moral outrage is always fairly amusing, but when it's laced

with the patronising righteousness of the liberal left it's very hard for me not to laugh out loud, and I've been laughing a lot this week, so thank you all very much indeed for that.

Some of you atheists were so hopping mad it wouldn't surprise me if you started to believe in God just to ensure there was no possibility of having anything at all in common with the likes of me. What can I say?

Well, I can respect anyone who disagrees with me politically, and I don't even mind a few insults, because I know political views are often held with great passion. But I think some people, in their eagerness to condemn me as a fascist, really only heard what they wanted to hear and missed the point of the video, which was to encourage people to vote for someone who actually shares their values in order to enhance our democracy and strengthen all our freedom, and to vote against those career politicians who want to take away our right to defend ourselves from them at the ballot box, the only defence we have. The clue was in the title, in case anybody missed it.

Of course, I realise democracy is a dirty word to many people on the left, so OK, I apologise if it shocked or offended anyone's delicate sensibilities or hurt their tender feelings. And I do hope you'll be able to find it in your hearts, once the pain has subsided, to forgive me for having had the temerity to vote with my conscience and not with yours. You see, for me this is a single-issue election, because without the right of self-determination all politics is merely an empty charade. You know, like we have at the moment.

Of course I don't agree with all UKIP policies any more than I do with any other party. So no, I'm not voting for climate change scepticism or for homeopathy or for antidisestablish-mentarianism (try saying that with a mouthful of marbles).

I'm voting for something that isn't on offer from any of the other parties, because it's a bit too democratic for them, and because they know very well what the outcome would be. I'm voting for a principle that would resonate with the authors of the American Constitution, one of the greatest documents ever written: the right of the people to decide who governs them, a right that has been taken away from us without permission and that I want to see restored. And it's by far the most important issue for me in this election. It's way more important than athe-ism or science or anything else, because it holds the key to our freedom.

Although I'm an atheist, my argument with religion has always been political, and not theological. I think debating whether or not God exists is about as pointless as arguing about football or *Star Trek* episodes. Everybody is right and everybody is wrong, and none of it matters.

What does matter is what people do with their beliefs, and the licence they take from them to behave in ways that impinge on other people's freedom is really what concerns me about reli-gion.

Yes, of course I think it's all nonsense, but if that's all it was I wouldn't have a problem with it. Unfortunately it's dangerous nonsense, because the privileged status we give religion out of respect for the spiritual is always exploited politically, especially by the two fascist religions of Christianity and Islam.

And right now in Britain, indeed all over Europe, Islam is being allowed to exploit it to the hilt, and beyond, by playing not only the religion card, but also the culture card and the race card, in a kind of three-card trick that intimidates us into censoring ourselves, lying to ourselves, and insulting our own intelligence in a way that disempowers us.

However, I think Islam is only a threat in the way a dangerous dog is a threat, when it's enabled by an irresponsible moron. And Islam is being enabled by the irresponsible politics of the multicultural left. And that's what I'm voting against.

So, in a nutshell, I'm voting for self-determination and against the multicultural left and every ugly cowardly little thing it stands for. And I'm not really paying very much attention to any of the other policies. They can all wait until the basics are fixed.

And yes, you can call it a protest vote, because that's what it is, for a protest party that wouldn't even need to exist if politicians had the courage to trust the people the way they're always asking the people to trust them, even though they've shown us repeatedly that they are not fit to be trusted.

And this seems to me a very lopsided arrangement, and it's why I'm trying to do my bit, however small, to correct it, and I urge you to do the same, because you may never get another chance. That's what I was saying in the previous video, and that's what I'm saying now.

So go on, go ahead, when you've finished all your whining, and do the right thing. Betray atheism and betray science for the sake of freedom, just this once – you know you really want to. And I'll see you on the other side of this election with a nice little video all about Jesus. What a relief.

68

No Mosque at Ground Zero

June 4, 2010

All you Americans who have been following the Islamisation of Europe from afar with horrified incredulity, if any of you are still nursing the cosy illusion that it could never happen in your country it's time to wake up and rub those sleepy eyes, because the moment of truth has arrived.

In case you haven't heard, there's a plan afoot to build a thirteen-storey Islamic centre and mosque a few yards from Ground Zero in New York – a plan that has been enthusiastically welcomed by politicians and civic leaders eager to show how tolerant they are at other people's expense. Is it possible to be astonished but not surprised?

Apparently it's not enough that nearly three thousand innocent people had to lose their lives in a hideous act of religious mass murder, but now their memory has to be insulted as well, and the religion that murdered them allowed to build a towering triumphalist mosque on the ground where they died. Is America losing its mind?

It says a lot about the people behind this scheme that they had the bad taste even to propose building a mosque in such a place, but to describe it, as they have, as a tribute to the victims is beyond bad taste and shows a profound contempt for those who died. It would be hard to imagine a more provocative gesture short of standing on their graves and burning the American flag. Yet how typical of Islam, with its own hair-trigger sensitivity to the slightest imagined insult, to do something so arrogant and so insensitive.

It's going to cost a hundred million dollars to build this thing, but nobody is prepared to say where the money is coming from. We do know the Saudis fund a lot of mosque-building in the West when they're not busy trying to stamp out free speech at the United Nations or telling Fox News what to broadcast, so I guess we'll all be paying for it every time we start the car.

It seems to me a much more appropriate place for a mosque in New York would be the United Nations building itself, because that organisation has become so Islamo-friendly in recent years that frankly I'm surprised it doesn't already have a minaret.

I'm not even American, but it makes me sick to my stomach to think that Islam is going to be allowed anywhere near Ground Zero, because 9/11 could never have happened if not for Islam and its teachings, its doctrine of jihad, and its false promise of an impossible afterlife, without which none of those gullible lunatics would have been persuaded to carry out such an insane act.

And also, because it wasn't just an attack on America, but on all of us in the civilised world; as were the bombings in London, Madrid, Bali, the shootings in Mumbai, and everywhere else the religion of peace decides it doesn't like the way people do things.

Any religion that endorses violence is incapable of delivering spiritual enlightenment (how obvious does that have to be?) and it has no right even to call itself a religion.

Without the shield of religion to hide behind, Islam would be banned in the civilised world as a political ideology of hate, and we have no obligation to make allowances for it, any more than we do for Nazism.

It's a bigger threat to our freedom than Nazism ever was. Yes, both are totalitarian, and both divide the world unnecessarily into us and them, the pure and the impure, and both make no secret of their desire to exterminate the Jews.

But we were all more or less on the same side against the Nazis, whereas the Islamo-Nazis have plenty of friends among people in the West who ought to know better. American politicians now regularly make the kind of dhimmi noises about diversity as an excuse for Islamisation, the same kind of thing we've become so depressingly familiar with in Europe.

It's true that diversity has been good for America. It's been the making of that country. But American diversity has always been grounded in respect for the values, the individual liberties, that make America what it is.

Islam rejects those values. That's the difference, and it's a very important difference. Islam despises what America is. It rejects everything America stands for, including freedom, and diversity, and any Muslim who denies that is a liar.

The organisation behind this scheme is called the Cordoba Initiative, and the building is to be called Cordoba House. This is because Córdoba is the city in southern Spain where Muslims built their first great mosque at the start of, and as a symbol of, their conquest of Spain.

The Ground Zero mosque is intended to serve the same purpose in America. Building mosques on conquered sacred ground is standard practice. It's what Islam has always done to assert its supremacy, and that is what's happening here.

And of course they know how insulting it is, how offensive it is, are you kidding? Why do you think they chose a site as close as possible to Ground Zero? Or do you think that was just an accident?

And they also know that once it's built it will be there forever, as a permanent affront to all Americans, gloating in triumph, and a major bridgehead in the ongoing stealth jihad. That's how the Muslim world will see it, and that's how they'll be encouraged to see it. And to be fair to them, that's exactly what it will be, confirming what they've always suspected, that America is a soft country, a decadent country, crippled by political correctness, confused and guilt-ridden, with no backbone and no pride.

They plan to open it next year on September 11th, the tenth anniversary of the atrocity. Is that tasteless enough for you? I'm surprised they haven't organised a 757 flypast.

But it doesn't have to be that way. Here in London we had a similar situation just recently where they wanted to build a gigantic mosque to overshadow the Olympic Games. Public opinion put a stop to that, and public opinion can put a stop to this disgraceful plan as well. And it can tell this group and the politicians who support them that enough is enough, and that this is one insult too far, and that America is a big country, and there's plenty of room for them to build their offensive mosque if they have to somewhere else – somewhere perhaps more appropriate to the spirit of their religion, like the Arizona desert, or Death Valley.

69

The Pope Needs a Miracle

June 27, 2010

We've all become quite used to hearing outrageous comments from the Pope, so when he said recently that a priest is a gift to the world the only real surprise was that he managed to say it with a straight face.

As if God said: "Hey world, I got a gift for you. I got it specially. It's a predatory class of self-serving parasites who will suck out your dreams and grind them to dust, who'll poison your naturally joyful and spontaneous nature with the leaden and life-draining emotions of guilt and fear, and who'll lead you away from the path of wisdom and enlightenment and straight into a box canyon of superstition and dogma solely for their benefit. And you're going to lap it up like puppy dogs. Any questions? No, I didn't think so. Well, just for that I'm going to let them rape your kids as well, and get away with it. Enjoy."

And by the way, even as the Pope was telling us that priests are a gift to the world, five Italian gifts to the world were being suspended by their bishops for the usual reasons.

Abolishing clerical celibacy, now that would be a gift to the world. Without it the Catholic Church is going to need a miracle to come back from this low point in its already ignominious history. And I do mean a genuine miracle. Something that changes reality, because I'm afraid words are no longer enough. Moral teaching is no longer enough when we can all plainly see that it's the men who run the Catholic Church who are most in need of some moral teaching of their own. In fact, some of them are in need of a severe moral kicking, and Pope Ratzinger is top of that list.

They call him the Holy Father, but his record shows that he wouldn't know holy if it spat in his eye. And if he is a father he's kept it quiet for professional reasons. He's shaping up to be the most conservative pope since... well, since the last one, and he was so conservative he virtually fossilised in office.

Back in those days this pope was the Vatican's chief enforcer of doctrine. His nickname was God's Rottweiler. Yet now we're supposed to believe that he's some kind of benign pastoral shepherd. Give me a break.

And it was in this role that he helped to organise the cover-up of the institutionalised child rape for which the Catholic Church will now always be notorious (without a miracle, that is).

I think the Catholic Church actually owes humanity a miracle. It has traded on miracles for two thousand years. It derives all its authority from miracles. In fact, without the miracles there wouldn't be anything there at all, apart from the foundation of poison guilt upon which the whole thing stands.

And if the Church ever needed a miracle, now certainly is that moment, so it wouldn't hurt the Pope at least to try. What has he got to lose, his virginity? He is supposed to be Christ's direct representative on earth. Surely some of that stardust has rubbed off.

Plus he's got a captive audience eager to believe. To the Catholic mind, if a thing isn't absolutely impossible it isn't worth believing in. The more impossible it is the more passionately it's believed. In fact, it's the impossibilities that keep this religion real. So if you're looking for something to believe, and if you have a taste for the gothically absurd and the horribly preposterous, then look no further than the Catholic faith, which can offer you a veritable smorgasbord of insulting nonsense on which to gorge, from the virgin birth right through to the resurrection and beyond – calling at all stations of the cross along the way.

The stations of the cross, as you may know, are a series of pictures around the walls of every Catholic church depicting, frame by frame, the torture and execution of Christ, because the Catholic faith likes to dwell on the suffering and the agony of Christ a lot more intensely than other Christian denominations. There's a real darkness about it that's almost satanic. No, actually I take that back – the world "almost", I mean.

A crucifix in a Catholic church will always show Jesus looking a lot more bloody and emaciated, because Catholicism really loves to relish the suffering, to get its teeth right into the flesh and to wallow in the blood of Christ. It's the nearest thing to outright Christian voodoo, frankly. The only thing missing is a decapitated chicken.

The most sacred thing a Catholic can do is to eat the flesh of Christ. The real flesh, not some synthetic substitute. And they can do this thanks to the miracle (what else?) of transubstantiation, which allows the Communion bread to magically transform itself into the actual flesh of Jesus Christ. Not symbolically, this is the crucial point, but in actual physical miraculous reality you take the living flesh of Christ right in your mouth as a Catholic, every single time. Yes you do, because Jesus said: "Eat my body and drink my blood, because you're nothing but a bunch of superstitious savages anyway, so you might as well act like it." (I'm paraphrasing, obviously, but I believe that was the gist of what he said, and if it wasn't it bloody well should have been.)

Obviously other Christian denominations take Communion, but the flesh of Christ is a particular staple of the Catholic diet. We Catholics know that if you don't take the flesh of Christ about once a week you're not really getting all your essential nutrients, which could lead to a grace deficiency and lower your immunity to possession by demons, for example; this is a very common occurence.

Oh yes, demonic possession is as big a threat to the Catholic soul as a Harry Potter book or a condom, so the church takes it very seriously. They've even trained a whole squad of exorcists, specialist demon hunters, to deal with this problem. The dog-collared ghostbuster is the demon's worst nightmare. (Well, probably not his worst nightmare because, after all, he lives in hell, but you know what I mean.) And these guys go around sprinkling holy water on people with mental problems who have forgotten to take their medication, while invoking the power of Christ.

But what puzzles me about this – well, many things puzzle me about it – but what puzzles me most is: if they can harness the power of Christ to drive out demons, which is what they claim to be doing, how come they can't use it for any other purpose, like, say, feeding a multitude?

This planet is never short of a starving multitude or two, yet for some reason the power of Christ always seems to be conspicuously absent. It can drive out demons all day long, it seems, yet when it comes to something we can actually verify, the power of Christ miraculously evaporates.

So wouldn't it be wonderful if the Pope could reassure us all (now that his church has been exposed to the world as a cesspit of iniquity, as a whited sepulchre inwardly teeming with rottenness and filth), if he could just reassure us that his religion isn't in fact a crock of superstitious fascist gobbledegook and lies, by demonstrating the power of Christ just once?

One little miracle. Think of the difference it would make to the Church's reputation, to everything. It would change reality. Suddenly all the Catholic miracles would become real. Think of the converts from all the other religions. Catholic churches packed to the rafters. Everybody singing "hallelujah". You never know, a host of heavenly angels might even appear.

Plus, of course, it would make it so much easier to persuade Catholic parents their children had been touched by the hand of God, and not by some creepy nonce in a dog collar.

Didn't Jesus himself say that anyone could do the things that he did if they had enough faith? Well, what is he waiting for? He does have enough faith. We know that, because he's the Pope.

So couldn't he at least go to a famine area with some loaves and fishes and see what happens? Isn't it even worth a shot? Or is human life not really all that sacred when you actually have

FREEDOM IS MY RELIGION

to get off your arse and account for yourself, and you think you
might be embarrassed? And did Jesus really sacrifice himself
on that bloody cross of death so that this pampered brazen old
fraud could sit there in Rome like a useless ornament telling
everybody else what they're not allowed to do?

His entire religion is built on black magic. It runs through
it like an electric current. Yet he is unable to demonstrate even
the simplest example of it when his Church most needs one. It's
odd, because they'll certainly find a miracle for him after he's
gone, when it's time to make him a saint. They'll have no trouble
then finding somebody prepared to swear they were healed by
his touch. I'm sure it has already been arranged.

70

The Enemy Within

July 18, 2010

It always amazes me how many people in the West would happily compromise the foundations of our entire civilisation to appease religious fascism. I find it disturbing that they would care so little about their children's future, even if they're too complacent, or naive, or politically blinkered to care about their own.

And one of the most depressing questions I get asked by people like this is: "Why do you hate Muslims?"

It's depressing because anyone who has seen my videos knows very well that I've never expressed hatred for anyone. Hate is for losers, we all know that, because it's self-destructive. (We do all know that, don't we?)

It's often claimed that many people in the West are converting to Islam, and it's true that some are. But it's also true that many Muslims in the West are leaving Islam, but you don't hear so much about them for obvious reasons.

Some of them have been brave enough to make themselves known and reach out to help other Muslims who want to escape the tyranny of their religion. And, like them, it's the religion I have a problem with, not the people.

So no, I don't hate Muslims, thanks for asking. I wish them well. Even the fanatics who stand at the roadside with their dopey little banners and bulging eyeballs calling for death to the West. I even wish those boneheads well in that I wish them good mental health, if that isn't too wildly optimistic.

And of course I know there are lots of moderate, peaceful Muslims. Indeed, many of them are so moderate and peaceful they're invisible and silent. And that's part of the problem. And just because there are lots of peaceful Muslims it doesn't mean the religion is not an aggressive fascist ideology that threatens all our freedom. Nor does it mean that western governments aren't falling over themselves to make excuses for it, pretending that Islam has nothing to do with the violence inspired and sanctioned by its scripture, and repeatedly carried out in its name.

Just look at the craven behaviour that allowed the massacre at Fort Hood to take place. We know it could have been prevented, but thanks to political correctness in the American army (the American army?!) all the warning signs were ignored in case somebody got offended.

All reference to Islam has been airbrushed out of the official Pentagon report, even though the guy handed out copies of the Koran beforehand and shouted "Allahu akbar" as he carried out the murders.

I'm surprised the officers who shot him haven't been accused of Islamophobia. Maybe they will be at the trial when we find out what a victim he is, and how, living in a decadent country like America, his religion is the only thing keeping him sane.

All over the western world we've given Islamic supremacists the impression that they have every right to be outraged, insulted and offended by everything we do and say. And some of us have come to believe it ourselves, and that is the real core of this problem.

Mark Twain said faith is believing what you know ain't so. Well, political correctness is doing what you know ain't right.

In every western country Islamic extremists are allowed to exploit religious privilege for political ends by claiming to represent all Muslims, and the media always treat them as if they do.

These groups give themselves official-sounding titles and talk a smooth line in community harmony, while doing all they can to prevent integration and to keep Muslims apart and ghettoised in a separate society with a separate identity, separate rules and standards.

In other words, they exist to cause division in society, to drive a wedge between communities that doesn't need to be there any more than they need to exist as organisations.

Take, for example, The Council on American-Islamic Relations. That's quite a puffed-up, important-sounding title that implies a meeting of equal ideologies, equal points of view that need to find common ground when, in fact, all that's needed is for Muslim immigrants to adapt to the American way of life, or the British or Australian or Canadian way of life, or not to go there; to respect the laws and customs like everyone else, not to try and change them to Islamic ones, and not to define themselves as a separate group deserving special status. That's where it begins and ends. There is no debate. There is no common ground to find. There is no American-Islamic relations, and there is no need for any self-appointed council of sharia-advocating Hamas-linked religious fascists to oversee it.

Sharia in the West is like urine in a water hole. Any amount is too much. Sharia dehumanises women. It threatens the freedom and dignity of every woman in the western world. It discriminates in such a fundamental way there's no way around it. There's no compromise. Misogyny runs through it like a dye. And that should be more than enough reason for us to banish it as aggressively and as thoroughly as we banish rabies.

If you live in the United States, and especially if you've ever accused anyone of Islamophobia, I urge you to read this book: *Muslim Mafia.**

If you read only one book this year, or one book in your whole life, make it this one for your sake and the sake of your children, especially the female ones.

This book is the result of an undercover investigation that reveals the bare-knuckle truth about CAIR, the Muslim Brotherhood, and the extensive network of Islamic fanatics who have eaten their way into American society like termites, and who seek to undermine it and destroy it from within.

It provides substantial documentary proof that Islamists have penetrated the highest levels of American politics and law enforcement in their quest to impose sharia on the United States and get

---

* I got a lot of flak for recommending this book because it was written and published by hardcore Christians, but I don't care if Satan himself published it in collaboration with the Vatican, I'm just glad somebody did. It's not a particularly good book, and I never intended to imply that, but it contains important information that affects all of us, both inside and outside the United States. The comment about reading only one book was directed at Americans who don't read books because they've got more important things to do (like watching TV while picking their nose) to wake them up to what is being allowed to take root in their society without their knowledge.

rid of the Constitution, aided and abetted by the most cowardly and shameful political correctness in government, in the media, and especially within the FBI, who seem to think it's more important to be culturally sensitive than to defend national security.

This is an important book, which is why the American media have so assiduously ignored it. In publishing it, the authors have done more for their country and the civilised world than all the politicians on Capitol Hill combined will achieve in their entire careers.

Political Islam is a threat to all civilised people; Muslims, Christians, Hindus, Sikhs, atheists, Buddhists, and especially Jews.

If America falls we all do. So wherever you live in the world, if you care about freedom, read this book and read it soon.

71

A God of Life

July 26, 2010

People sometimes tell me: "I kind of agree with you about religion, but you can be a bit negative. You should be more positive."

Okey-dokey.

I'm positive that organised religion is irredeemably evil, I'm positive it exists for the sole benefit of professional clergy, and I'm positive that the only way it can possibly survive is by glorifying ignorance and brainwashing children, which I'm positive violates their human rights.

I'm positive that the spiritual guidance you'll receive from a professional clergyman is on a par with the medical attention you'd have got from a thirteenth-century doctor, and that finding the meaning of life in organised religion is about as likely as finding a pub in Saudi Arabia called the Shoplifter's Arms.

I'm positive that the more we allow clerical opinion to influence public life the closer we get to totalitarianism. Religion's history, past and present, proves this beyond any doubt.

But most of all I'm positive that if we put as much effort

into engaging with reality as we do in trying to escape from it through religion, we might find out a bit more about it, and that would be very positive for all of us, except of course for professional clergy, who depend on our fear and ignorance for their very existence, and to whom, therefore, knowledge, wisdom or any kind of human enlightenment is about as welcome as a dose of the pox.

The most genuinely positive thing I can say about religion is that it's a triumph of the human imagination. But it's also proof that there is no idea so absurd or self-destructive that we aren't capable of enthusiastically talking ourselves into it. And I don't know what this is. Maybe it's some kind of biological need we have to do this to ourselves, to pretend we've connected with something greater than ourselves, to cheapen it with bone-headed ignorance and righteous hypocrisy and then to ram it down each other's throats. Maybe that's what we're here to do in this life because, if it is, we can count ourselves a huge success. (That's quite positive. Maybe not.)

There are many things I don't understand about religion, as people never tire of telling me. For example, why somebody would kneel in a church asking to be delivered from evil. Why go in there in the first place?

Or why, if God is really so all powerful and merciful, he doesn't simply forgive Satan, and none of this nonsense would be necessary. Why can't he let that happen? What is he afraid of? You have to wonder, don't you?

But the thing I find most difficult to understand is, if you have to worship a god, and clearly some people do, why choose a god of death, a god who wants you to hate yourself, who wants you to deliver yourself to him as a broken thing with wounds that need healing, and to inflict those wounds yourself? It just doesn't make sense. And I know it's not supposed to make sense and that's what faith is all about, but this doesn't make sense on an "are you insane?" level. Especially when you've got a ready-made god of life shining its light on the planet every day, because the sun actually is the source of all life on this earth; our creator and our salvation, you might say. And it's the nearest thing to a real god we're ever going to have. Without it, this planet would be just a ball of dead rock flying around on its own in the dark; you know, like an Islamist's braincell.

If you're a Christian, you might as well worship the sun, because you do anyway; you just don't know it. Christianity is really nothing more than astrology with attitude. The entire Jesus story has been lifted wholesale from the sun god myth, and not for the first time either. There are many other holy figures with exactly the same life story as Jesus, right down to the details. The virgin birth, the star in the east, the twelve apostles, the miracles, the crucifixion, the resurrection, and so on and so on. The story has been told and retold time and time again, and it's all been inspired by the sun, the one true god.

"Ah," you say, "what about morality? The sun can't impart a sense of morality."

Well, what a bonus that is, because the morality imparted by the god of death is not a morality at all. It's a raft of threats. Obey or be punished. That's no morality, and knuckling under to it has no virtue. It's the behaviour of a trained animal. So you can put that morality where the sun doesn't shine, wherever that might be. I'll take the golden rule because it makes rational sense, and I'll take it in the sun. And maybe you should as well.

Admittedly the sun is no more than a giant ball of burning gas, so whatever consciousness it may possess is unlikely to respond to your prayers directly, but you're already used to that.

And we know the sun is actually there. We don't need to speculate about that or take anything on trust from people with their own agenda who don't know any more than we do, and who, in many cases, know considerably less.

We can feel the sun's warmth and we can see its light breathing life into everything that lives. What more do you want from a god? Popcorn?

And all we have to do is celebrate it. There's no punishment, no guilt, and best of all no professional clergy. It doesn't get any more positive than that.

72

Freedom Is My Religion

August 2, 2010

I'd like to clear up something once and for all, if I may, because from the correspondence I've received, it's clear that a number of people in what's called the "atheist community" have taken exception to some of my opinions and no longer consider me one of their own. Apparently I've violated some kind of atheist orthodoxy, and I've been, for want of a better word, excommunicated. And I have to say that really is quite an honour. Thank you very much indeed. I feel so liberated now I could almost go into a church and give thanks. Almost.

If I cared what atheists thought about me I'd never be able to bring myself to say a critical word about Islam. And that's what I think about the "atheist community".

You see, I've noticed that many atheists are very happy to attack Christianity with the full force of their finely honed intellects, driving home their arguments like fence posts, yet when it comes to Islam it's a different story. Suddenly atheism takes a back seat and political correctness steps forward, and the argument gets inverted like an hourglass, with the sand running in the opposite direction as they rush to find excuses for religious fascism and to condemn anyone who speaks against it as a racist.

(What about all the Hindus and Sikhs I hear from who feel the same way about Islam, are they racists as well?)

Atheists pride themselves on examining the evidence, yet too often when evidence to do with Islam is presented it's filtered through political correctness and rendered inadmissible, because there seems to be a default assumption that drawing attention to the ongoing soft jihad against western values (that's soft like a velvet hammer) is somehow a slander on Muslims, that the religion is essentially benign, and that its critics are motivated primarily by bigotry and hate.

I've encountered this attitude so many times now I'm no longer surprised by it, but I think the people who are afflicted with it are as much in denial as any religious bigot. They're equally irrational, equally delusional. They're just slaves to a different dogma.

I'm an atheist, but I don't love atheism. However, I do love freedom. I've said before that freedom is my religion, and I wasn't joking (because we all know you should never joke about something as solemn and sacred as religion).

I don't worship freedom because I don't worship anything, but I do regard it as the highest virtue and the one from which all other virtues spring. And, of course, it's extremely un-Islamic, which, between you and me, is one of the best things about it. But don't tell anyone I said that, as I would hate to cause disharmony.

I'm a fairly recent convert to the religion of freedom. Most of my life I've taken freedom for granted. It has just been there in the background being reliable and boring, but since the rise of the European superstate, along with multiculturalism, the religion of peace and all the insane bollocks that goes with it, I'm pleased to say that my appreciation for freedom as a concept has been fully awoken and has now reached genuinely religious proportions. Hallelujah.

It isn't the usual kind of religion, admittedly, as it doesn't require anyone to think less of themselves, which might be a problem for somebody who believes there's virtue in self-hatred. Nor does it preach hatred of any group of people like, for example, homosexuals or Jews, which will obviously limit its appeal among those of the single braincell persuasion. But if you measure religious conviction by strength of belief (and why shouldn't you?) then freedom is definitely my religion, and I warmly recommend it to any atheists who may be looking for something tangible and worthwhile to believe in, as clearly some of them are.

The reason I make videos can be summed up in three words: Freedom From Religion. And, given the way the world is right now, inevitably that means especially freedom from the religion of peace. And if that makes me a bigot or a racist or a fascist or a hate-monger or any of the other choice names I've been called by atheists, then so be it. I'll just have to wear it, because I don't actually have a choice.

You see, Islam rejects individual freedom, and therefore in accordance with my deeply and sincerely held convictions I'm obliged to reject Islam, which I do unequivocally. It is, to borrow a term, haram to me. I avoid it the way a Muslim avoids pork.

To hear someone advocate the obscenity of sharia is as offensive to me as it would be to Muslims if I were to stroll into my local mosque during Friday prayers handing out bottles of beer and bacon sandwiches.

However, I believe that Islam wouldn't be the problem it is today in the western world, and sharia wouldn't even be an issue, if not for the grossly irresponsible self-indulgence of cultural guilt and political correctness which I believe has literally turned us into our own worst enemies. It's the rot in the foundations of western society through which the poison of religious fascism is being allowed to seep, and if we carry on as we are, making ludicrous allowances for it, mollycoddling hate, tolerating intolerance, and looking for excuses to make excuses for Islam, our society will be poorer for it and our children will be less free – especially the female ones. And history will condemn us as the generation of liars and cowards that let it happen; the generation that was morally and politically so far up its own rectum it didn't even notice the lights going out.

And I don't want that on my conscience, thank you very much. I don't want to be the person who wishes they'd said something when they had the chance. And frankly the last thing on my mind is what atheists may or may not think about it.

73

The Faith of Idiots

August 7, 2010

Christianity has been around for two thousand years, and during that time it has attracted its fair share of idiots.

It sounds a long time, two thousand years, but it's nothing compared with the age of the planet, which is, of course, an astonishing six thousand years. (How can anyone even imagine such a number?)

Of course, not everyone who has religious faith is a complete idiot, but a lot of stupid people do have faith because they're stupid, for the simple reason that believing is a hell of a lot easier than thinking.

It takes time and effort to acquire knowledge, whereas any fool can acquire faith instantly and effortlessly. If it took effort most people wouldn't bother with it. That's why it's all about lazy stuff – submission, surrender, don't ask questions, let your moral values be handed to you on a plate like a baby. Let ignorance be your crowning virtue, so that every piece of rational truth or common sense that comes your way becomes a test for your faith, and the more you resist the more virtuous you are. Let that faith swell up inside your mind like an airbag, pushing out everything else, and then all your questions will be answered. Isn't that reassuring? No wonder faith is so popular.

But how far does faith have to be stretched before it becomes just pure unadulterated dumb stupidity? When does embracing religion become the equivalent of undergoing an operation to have your IQ lowered?

You may be familiar with the expression: "God said it. I believe it. That settles it."

It's popular with the bumper-sticker Christians, the creationist cracker-barrel sages of the American Bible Belt, who find it useful as a kind of crude theological straight arm.

It's an expression I've heard a few times, and each time I've marvelled at the imbecility of anyone who could even think it, let alone display it on their vehicle, but until this week I had never actually received it in an email, especially not one where it constituted the entire text: "God said it. I believe it. That settles it."

To be fair it is actually a masterpiece of concision. Acres of impenetrable theological bullshit have been whittled down to a simple pithy definition of what faith actually is.

When you strip away all the pretentious hogwash about transcendence and all the other flimflam, that's what you're actually left with, those nine little words of final judgment, beyond reason and beyond doubt.

If spoken, ideally they should be declaimed loudly, repeatedly, and with fingers in ears, because this is a statement designed to be worn like a brass plate on the forehead announcing: "This mind is closed for business. We are not currently accepting any new ideas, thank you for your interest, because God said it, we believe it, that settles it."

The person who sent this email neglected to sign it, so I don't know who they are, but I do know what they are. What kind of gullible muttonhead would you have to be to make that statement in public and actually mean it? You might as well be walking around with a bucket over your head inviting people to strike it with a hammer to try and kick-start your brain, you dumb ignorant Christian shitkicker.

No offence, but those of us who don't believe that Jesus rode around on a dinosaur would be more inclined to the view that God didn't say it, you're a complete moron, and that settles it, if you don't mind me saying so, and even if you do.

74

An Irish Joke

August 17, 2010

Do you find yourself getting offended by people who get offended? It seems to me that these days more and more people are choosing to be offended in a quite opportunistic way about the most trivial, inconsequential things, and I find that offensive. Can I get compensation?

I just read a story in the English press about an oversensitive Irishman who collected thousands in compensation because somebody told him a joke he found objectionable. That's right, a joke.

Not a particularly funny joke. An Irishman is sitting in a pub with an empty beer glass and somebody asks him if he wants another one, to which he responds: "Why would I want another empty glass?"

I know. Tumbleweed.

Yet one sad individual claimed to be so offended by this non-joke he felt the need to make an official complaint about it, and after two years of legal wrangling he finally got his money.

I'm not a particular fan of the Irish joke, but I think people like this are a very good reason to actively preserve the Irish joke and ensure that it lives forever.

I was born in Ireland and raised in England, so I was subjected to Irish jokes the entire time I was growing up. I never took it seriously enough to be offended because I thought some of them were quite funny, I realised they had nothing to do with me personally, and, of course, there was no money involved back then. Nowadays you get the distinct impression that some people actively go looking to be offended because they know there will be a generous payout, thanks to the twisted values of a supremely sick society that encourages a "poor me" mentality of phoney victimhood at every turn.

As for Irish jokes, to my mind there is no more offensive an Irish joke than the super-sensitive Paddy who takes offence for money. I do hope that doesn't offend.

I've known quite a lot of Irish people in my time, and I'm just wondering now if maybe I know this guy from somewhere.

I'm wondering if he's the same Irishman I heard about who went to the dentist to have a wisdom tooth put in.

Or if he's the Irishman who fell out the window while ironing the curtains. It would be quite a coincidence if he was.

Or maybe he's the Irishman who thought a sheet of sandpaper was a map of the desert, or the Irishman who went to a mind reader and got his money back, or the one who took a tape measure to bed to see how long he slept. Or maybe he's the Irishman who put ice cubes in his condom to keep the swelling down.

If so, his name is definitely Paddy, even if it isn't (especially if it isn't). And, depending on how we're feeling about it, he may well be smoking a clay pipe, wearing a jaunty little bowler hat, and carrying a pig under his arm. And he's very unlikely to be sober.

And, if his ears are burning now, the phone must have rung while he was ironing again. Jesus, Mary and Joseph, what a stupid fecking eejit, what a thick Irish mick.

75

Bad Faith at Ground Zero

August 28, 2010

It seems the Ground Zero mosque project has succeeded in dividing America like a shovel going through a pumpkin. Even the president has an opinion. Well, kind of an opinion. And now the story has gone worldwide. Everybody is waiting to see what happens. We all know that if Islam can get away with a stunt like this in America it can get away with anything.

People keep framing this as a religious freedom issue, but there's a difference between practising your religion, which everyone has the right to do, and rubbing your religion in people's faces as a triumphalist political statement, which is what's happening here.

I'd be interested to know just how bad an insult has to be before it's no longer protected by the First Amendment.* After all, the Second Amendment gives Americans the right to bear arms, but in practice you need a permit to walk around packing

---

* This comment referred to the religious freedom aspect of the First Amendment, not to free speech, which I support unequivocally for everyone without exception.

99

hardware and not everybody can get one, despite the Second Amendment.

Also, I can't help wondering if Mayor Bloomberg's unwavering support for this project is less about his commitment to religious freedom and more about his business interests in Dubai, where his company is attempting to establish itself as a major provider of sharia financial services in the Middle East. Maybe somebody should ask him.

Liberal commentators keep telling us this is not really a mosque at all. It's just a community centre and prayer room, and it isn't even at Ground Zero.

Well, a mosque is both a community centre and a prayer room, and the mosque part of this building will occupy the top two floors, which means it will overlook the scene of conquest, which is why the site was chosen.

When the governor of New York offered to help them find an alternative site they wouldn't even discuss it. Moving it somewhere else would negate the very purpose of building it, which is to rub 9/11 in America's face. If they can't build it there, there's no point in building it anywhere else.

Nobody knows where the money is coming from, and nobody wants to say. The developer was waiting tables five years ago, and now he's spending millions in cash on a building in downtown Manhattan. He must have had some very generous tippers.

As for the supposedly moderate imam behind it, he supports sharia, he supports the Iranian theocracy, he won't condemn terrorism, not even the exploitation of children as suicide bombers, and he blames America for 9/11. And now we hear he's even taking credit for Obama's speech in Cairo, of all things.

You remember, where he sucked up to the Muslim world and called it statesmanship.

If that's true, that's a hell of a lot of influence to have. I wonder if he had anything to do with the president's recent Ramadan speech where he praised Islam's role in "advancing justice, progress, tolerance and the dignity of all human beings".

Yes, President Obama actually said those words, and with a straight face. No wonder so many Americans think he's a Muslim. That's the kind of thing only a Muslim could say, or a European politician.

We all know how badly the president wants to be popular in the Muslim world, so I guess he felt he had to say something nice because his audience was full of Islamic activists who might otherwise have accused him of Islamophobia and racism and forced him to undergo cultural awareness and sensitivity training, and how embarrassing would that be for the first black president?

But whoever provided him with that PC garbage ought to be fired on the spot, because it makes Obama sound as if he has no respect for the intelligence of the American people, which is as good as saying he wants to be a one-term president.

Everybody knows that Islam has done absolutely nothing for justice, progress, tolerance or the dignity of human beings. Is he kidding? The worst thing you could do is expose any of those things to the influence of Islam, and to claim otherwise is simply a barefaced lie.

Doesn't he realise nobody is buying this crap any more? He must have seen the opinion polls. He must know that there are millions of people all over the free world who simply don't trust this religion any more, because time and again they've seen its activists exploiting our freedoms to act in bad faith, exactly as they're doing at Ground Zero. They've seen that when it comes to Islam the tolerance and respect only ever go one way.

A religion of peace? No. What people see, and have seen for twenty years since the Rushdie affair, is a religion of intolerance, of aggression, of phoney manufactured grievances and hysterical bullying, unreasonable and manipulative special pleading and privilege-seeking, gross misogyny, homophobia, anti-Semitism and violence. Anyone who speaks out against this religion can expect to be threatened with physical violence. Everything about it is confrontational. That's why it's unwelcome in the West, because it has made itself unwelcome. And that's what President Obama should have told those Islamic activists if he wants to call himself any sort of leader of the free world. And he also should have told them this mosque is making their religion even more unwelcome, so building it has got to be one of the stupidest things any Muslim could want to do, unless they were acting in bad faith, and in this case they most certainly are.

But that's no reason for idiots to go around abusing and assaulting people because they happen to be Muslim (as has happened a few times recently), because this issue is causing consternation among Muslims as well, some of whom, to their credit, have actually spoken out against it and condemned it as unnecessarily provocative. And predictably one woman who did so at a meeting in New York was afterwards threatened over the phone. Classy.

Still, if nothing else good comes out of this mess, at least it has given PC liberals the chance to stand up for something for a change, which must be quite a bracing experience for some of them. And I'm sure they're all delighted to know that it looks as if this thing will go ahead because obviously nothing can be done legally to stop it, and the people behind it clearly don't have the intelligence or good grace to withdraw the plans, even though they know as well as everyone else that if the positions were reversed and if this level of calculated insult was being directed at Islam there's no way on earth this project would be allowed to proceed, Constitution or no Constitution.

76

Drunk on Religion

September 6, 2010

In the past I've had some harsh words to say about Islam, but to be fair I've never had any Muslims actually knock on my door to try and convert me to their religion. I only wish I could say the same for Christians.

About three or four times a year they come around. It's usually Jehovah's Witnesses, sometimes Catholics or Mormons or God knows what else, and I used to engage them in conversation and debate about the issues, even inviting them in on occasion, until one time two Mormons came in and they were so aggressively stubborn about everything I had to literally threaten to beat them up to get them to leave, and since then evangelists have been about as welcome and as interesting to me as a brick through the window.

Besides, years ago I used to work with some Jehovah's Witnesses from whom I learned the art of arguing endlessly in circles. It's a talent I still possess, though I try to use it wisely – i.e. not at all, because you always come back to the same place, the brick wall we know as the Bible.

The Bible is true because it says it's true, and because it's the Bible it must be true. And round and round and round we go. I feel dizzy now just thinking about it.

I think it's ironic that Alcoholics Anonymous use religion to get people off booze, because I think religion is quite a lot like hard liquor. Some people can handle it and some clearly can't. And those who can't, well, they can be inclined to make a public spectacle of themselves. And that's because religion is very powerful stuff. I think it's a lot more powerful than we're prepared to admit. I think it's mind-altering stuff that affects people's behaviour in the most humiliating way, often.

Just imagine, for example, if your god told you to drink a bottle of whisky every day for breakfast, what a different person you'd be on the back of that little sacrament.

I think evangelising your religion door to door is like a drunken alcoholic going around with a bottle of whisky urging people to drink from it, and thinking that they themselves are some kind of advertisement for this activity.

Whenever I answer the door to Christians I find myself feeling involuntarily sorry for them, for the wretched pitiful state they've allowed themselves to be reduced to by this mind virus. I always feel like asking them why on earth I would want anything to do with a religion that does this to people.

I believe in certain things quite strongly, some things very strongly, but I wouldn't dream of going around knocking on doors, interrupting people's dinner to tell them about it (especially if I knew they had probably heard it a thousand times before), because that strikes me as a good way to make enemies – especially when they've got the nerve to pretend they've come round to share some good news: "Have you heard the good news?" (I thought nobody really said that, but they do.)

Obviously, as soon as I noticed the Bibles they were carrying I had a ballpark idea of what this good news was likely to be, and I wasn't disappointed. Or rather I was disappointed, because normally if somebody asks me if I've heard the good news my reaction is likely to be: "Great, I love good news, but wait, let me guess what it is. Let's see now, the Pope has been impeached? That would be good news. No? That is a shame, isn't it? We live in hope. I know, President Ahmadinejad of Iran has come out publicly as gay and had himself stoned to death? Not that either? Oh dear, what a disappointment. Ah, I've got it, the Organisation of Islamic Conference has been officially declared a terrorist organisation? No? Now that one really does surprise me. Still, it's only a matter of time, isn't it?

"OK, I give up. You might as well tell me. What's the good news? Oh but wait, before you do, it's not Jesus again, is it? Tell me oh tell me it's not Jesus again. It is? It's Jesus again? You have disappointed me. I was so looking forward to some genuinely good news, but it's just this stuff again, this fatuous puerile guilt-laden fantasy fairy-tale story of Jesus, this insulting garbage again. That's what you call good news? Are you sick? That's a silly question. Of course you're sick, and you should see a doctor."

That's what I should have said. However, what I did say was: "I've been thinking about this issue lately, because you two aren't the first people to knock on my door with a similar proposition. And based on the accumulated evidence I've seen standing on this doorstep, I've concluded that Christianity is simply too high a price to pay for eternal salvation, and therefore I have elected to forfeit my eternal soul and go directly to hell. So you can cross me off your list of potential sunbeams for Jesus in the happy knowledge that you will never have to knock on this door again. Isn't that good news?"

But answer came there none because they were already half-way down the street, and for me that was very good news, which I believe was the original point of the exercise, so everyone was a winner.

77

God or Nothing

October 25, 2010

OK, this video is for those people who have told me they believe in God for just about the stupidest reason I've ever heard, because, as they put it, you have to believe in something; you can't just believe in nothing.

Can't you? Oh dear. I wish somebody had told me earlier. Oh well.

So it's either the supernatural or it's nothing? What are you, hypnotised?

Anyway, if you only believe because you don't want to believe in nothing then surely you already believe in nothing; you're just pretending you don't. I'm sorry, I didn't mean to frighten anyone.

Maybe you think believing in nothing will plunge you into some kind of existential void; a bottomless chasm of uncertainty, perhaps? Not to worry. That's what we call an open mind.

I don't believe in nothing. I wouldn't know where to begin. I believe in lots of things. It's just that religion isn't one of them, because I've examined religion quite closely and I've found its version of reality to be false, insulting and degrading. I've also found its implementation to be sinister, coercive, fraudulent and grossly immoral, especially with regard to children.

You see, one thing I do believe is that to indoctrinate a child with the bigotries of religion is a predatory assault on an unformed mind. It's an act of sabotage, a mental circumcision that ought to be against the law. One day it will be, and then the term "human rights" might actually start to mean something.

However, if we're talking about the bigger picture, about where we come from and why we're here and so on, even there I wouldn't say I believe in nothing. I simply don't know the answer to those questions any more than you do. And I know you haven't got a clue about them because you're a human being, just like me.

I suppose the difference is I don't really mind not knowing. If the information should present itself that would be great, but I'm more concerned with enjoying the experience as it happens than I am in fretting about the possible cause of it, and I'm certainly not interested in making up childish fantasies to cling to like pieces of driftwood because I'm afraid I might go crazy if I believe in nothing.

Admitting that you don't know something is not the same as believing in nothing. Pretending you do know when you don't is much closer to believing in nothing, because, when you believe falsehood against all reason, truth has no way in.

Of course some religious people use reason when it suits them. They say things like: "If God didn't create everything, then who did? It couldn't just come from nothing. That's irrational."

Yes, we wouldn't want to be irrational, would we? People might get the idea that we were crazy.

Well, according to Stephen Hawking everything did come from nothing, so there. He says the universe can be explained without the need for a creator, because the laws of physics allow for it. But then what does he know next to a theologian?

I don't know if science does have all the answers, but I'm pretty sure that religion doesn't have any of them, especially when I look at some of the people who run it.

Religion was a pretty crude way of explaining reality even back in the days when we thought the earth was the centre of the universe. Now the universe isn't even the centre of the universe, to hear some people tell it. Now they're talking about a multiverse where our universe is just one of billions, like one tiny bubble in an ocean of bubbles. But of course the god of the Middle-Eastern desert on planet earth still created all of it, that goes without saying (when he wasn't busy laying down the law about shellfish and pork, obviously).

I have heard it said that the meaning of life may be found one day somewhere in the area between physics and philosophy, whatever that's supposed to mean. Between splitting atoms and splitting hairs, maybe.

Why not? I'd be open to that. Science has already shown us so much that boggles the imagination and that, frankly, doesn't make any rational sense that, when it comes to reality, I wouldn't rule anything out. Particle physics, for example, has revealed that this world of ours that we thought was solid isn't solid, yet we still appear to be here in all our corporeal reality. How can this possibly be?

Beats me.

Unless…

Yes, of course. You beat me to it, didn't you? Maybe it's a miracle. It's obvious when you think about it. A miracle would explain it. Miracles are great. They can explain anything. You believe in miracles, don't you? Yes, of course you do. Because you're a human being, and you have to believe in something, right? You can't just believe in nothing. That way lies madness, which can drive a person crazy, so they say.

Yes, a miracle makes sense to me. But then I am something of an ignoramus, so a miracle is actually very helpful to me because it enables me to hold strong absolutist opinions about things without the need to actually know or understand anything. And, predictably I suppose, it makes me sympathetic to the idea that knowing and understanding things should be blasphemy, a neat trick that enables me to drag everybody else down to my level of crass and wilful ignorance without having to make any kind of intellectual investment whatsoever. Yes, I thought you'd be impressed. And if anyone should challenge me on it I can simply accuse them of hate speech and shut them up quicker than a cow's arse in fly time. So, as you can see, I've got it all covered. Praise the Lord.

Meanwhile, back in the real world, do you want the truth? (You do want the truth, don't you?) The truth is nobody knows why we're here. Nobody. Not you, not me, not the priest, not the imam, not the scientist, nobody. And anyone who expresses an opinion on the subject is guessing. And your guess is as good as mine, or the Pope's, or Stephen Hawking's or anybody else's. And I think that anyone who insists that their guesswork is the truth and the only truth is a liar or a fool or both, and should be treated as such, not humoured and indulged as they presently are, and made to feel that there's virtue in their arrogance, but openly mocked and ridiculed. And if it hurts their feelings, so much the better. Not because I believe in gratuitous insult, I don't, but I do believe in responding to it in kind, and there is a difference.

As for you, if the fear of believing in nothing, the terror of an open mind, is keeping you in thrall to this monstrous crude imaginary god foisted on you by a class of parasitical fear-mongering clergy, this vengeful punisher who'll be waiting for you at the moment of death (looking forward to that?), then I would suggest for your own mental health you're far better off believing in nothing. Even if you do go crazy, you'll still be ahead of the game.

78

Free Speech in Europe

November 10, 2010

Europe today is a shining example to the whole world of how to piss in your own drinking water.

All over this continent, laws are being passed to stifle free speech, and people are being criminalised for speaking their mind.

Later this month in Austria, Elisabeth Sabaditsch-Wolff goes on trial accused of "denigrating religious teachings", a charge straight out of the Inquisition.

Her crime? Pointing out the passage in the Koran that allows a man to beat his wife. For this she faces the prospect of three years in prison. Welcome to justice, Eurabia style.

Meanwhile, I hear that some Dutch politicians are worried about their country's international reputation now the Freedom Party is involved in government. Well, they shouldn't worry. Their country's reputation couldn't be any lower than it is right now, thanks to them, and thanks to a crooked law that allows the country's most popular politician to be dragged into court like a criminal for telling the truth, in front of a panel of clearly biased judges who have since proven incapable of conducting a simple star chamber show trial because they don't have the wisdom or self-discipline to keep their partiality to themselves. At the very moment when the eyes of the world were on Dutch justice, the crooked judges of Amsterdam rose to the occasion and gave such a masterclass in wretched incompetence and bias, the trial had to be abandoned. Clearly more concerned with ideology than with justice, they've proven themselves unfit to judge a baby show.

One of them even had the nerve to accuse Mr Wilders of undermining the judiciary, but frankly, they don't need his help when they're doing such a fine job themselves of undermining not just the entire Dutch legal system, but the very foundations of western civilisation.

The prosecution don't want to proceed. They say there's no charge to answer, but the judges are pushing ahead anyway with a new trial because they're determined to get this guy.

You see, impartial justice was never the purpose of this trial, or the one in Austria. The purpose is to silence dissent by example. To show everyone else that they too will be treated as a common criminal if they dare to express a negative opinion about the world's most backward, intolerant and violent religion.

This is where we are in Europe today. It's like something out of the old Soviet Union. I'm surprised they haven't tried to incarcerate Mr Wilders in a mental hospital. Maybe that's yet to come.

To make matters worse, and quite a lot worse too, we have to contend not only with crooked judges and spineless lawmakers, but lazy and partisan journalists who corrupt the language to suppress the truth and who slander anyone who speaks up for western values as "far-right", as a fascist, a hate-monger and a racist, which is what far-right means.

The truth is that in Europe today the left is very much the new far-right. And this manifests most crudely here in Britain in a motley rabble of anti-democratic cultural self-haters, relativists, pimply-faced students, Islamists, anti-Semites and left-wing fascists who comprise the ironically named Unite Against Fascism organisation, whose tactic of choice is to bring violence to peaceful demonstrations they don't agree with like a bunch of jackbooted Nazi thugs, because they're afraid of free speech and they know they're defending the indefensible.

Unite against fascism, but not religious fascism, because that might offend the fascists. Perish the thought. But don't worry, you people don't need to be ashamed of yourselves (as if you'd know how) because the rest of us are busy doing it for you with interest.

And this kind of thing is happening all over Europe now. Anyone who stages a peaceful demonstration in favour of democracy or western values can expect to be physically attacked by gangs of these violent self-righteous dipsticks who owe their own freedom to other people's willingness to defend it, but whose own meagre horizons stretch only as far as the suppression of legitimate dissent. How very progressive.

Of course, these people are not really anti-fascist at all, are they? They're anti-freedom, anti-free thought, anti-free speech, anti-free everything except free handouts from the state.

You see, leftists and Islamists share a keen sense of entitlement from a society they affect to despise. So they're united in hypocrisy as well as in intolerance, ignorance, stupidity and hate.

115

Multiculturalism in Europe is dead in the water, as every recent election has shown. Even the politicians are admitting it now. Some people still cling to the illusion of it the way the Soviets clung to the illusion of Communism, but it's over, and these show trials and violent street attacks are symptoms of its death throes. They're the desperate acts of desperate people who have totally lost their way.

Criminalising opinion is an open admission that lawmakers have lost control and created a situation they can't handle. But that's what happens when the people are never asked for their opinion, and when they give it it's ignored.

Well, now it can't be ignored, and it won't be ignored. Whatever happens at these two trials, this is just the beginning. The genie is out of the bottle in Europe, and no multicultural diversity fascist is going to put it back.

Already thousands of people are speaking out and making their voices heard in opposition to the relentless Islamisation of our society, and soon it's going to be millions. People who have had enough of political correctness, of being told what they're allowed to think and say, and of being told to respect a religion that respects absolutely nobody.

And they're finding out, as they do speak out, that they're not alone, and that they're not, in fact, fascists and hate-mongers and racists at all, despite what they're told time and again by a cowardly, crooked press.

And, like many of those people, I oppose Islam for the simple reason that Islam opposes me and everything I believe in. I don't care how Muslims feel about that. I don't care how anyone feels about it. Nor should I be required to.

In my opinion, Islam's disgusting treatment of women is a crime against humanity, nothing less. It's a thousand percent wrong. There is no grey area. It's unconscionable and unforgivable. And it's poisoning the whole world. It's not different or relative. It's backward and uncivilised. There's no excuse for it, and no excuse for defending it.

This is what I believe, very strongly indeed. And you may disagree, and you have a right to do, just as I have a right to say so, and I do insist upon the right to say so as openly, as often and as loudly as I like, and anyone who chooses to be offended by it can go ahead and drop dead for all I care, with all due respect – especially over there in the Islamic republic of Austria.

Curbing free speech is like taxing air. Nobody has the right to do it, no matter who they are, or who they think they are, or what fancy badge they're wearing, or what holy book they're holding in their grubby little hand. So they can pass all the laws they like, and they can string them all together in a paper chain if they want to, or fly them like flags from the minaret of every mosque. Those laws will be resisted and they will be overturned, because they're the laws of cowards and appeasers whose rotten multicultural lie will soon be nothing more than an embarrassing stain on history. And the sooner the better, if I may say so.

79

Human Rights Travesty

November 19, 2010

I understand that some bedbugs have been found in the United Nations building in New York, which is unfortunate, but some good may come of it. You never know, maybe somebody could find a place for them on the Human Rights Council. They might help to elevate the integrity of that forum somewhat.

Yes, it's that time of year again, when members of the cartel of third world dictatorships known as the Organisation of Islamic Conference take time out from brutalising their own people to force through a resolution at the Human Rights Council against what they call the defamation of religions, by which they mean telling the truth about Islam and the countries where it calls the shots.

They say they want to stop people wrongly associating their religion with terrorism and human rights violations, but I don't think anyone does. I think people correctly associate Islam with those things. I certainly do, but then what do I know? All I've got to go on is overwhelming evidence.

Also, at the risk of sounding like a racist xenophobic hate-mongering Nazi fascist bigot, it does seem to me that allowing Islamic countries on to a human rights council is like having a bunch of mafiosi on a parole board. They've already made it perfectly clear that human rights don't apply to them if they conflict with sharia, which, of course, they always do, because civilisation conflicts with sharia.

In a sane world, these countries wouldn't even be allowed to look in the direction of a human rights council, let alone serve on one.

We're talking about places like Saudi Arabia, where you can be executed for witchcraft and where pubescent girls are married off to middle-aged perverts incapable of forming a normal relationship because of their religion; or Iran, which executes children, and where you can be stoned to death for getting into the wrong relationship; or Sudan, where slavery is practised by Muslims over non-Muslims, where the government has murdered millions of its own people, and where the president is an indicted war criminal.

We're talking about places dominated by bloodthirsty clerics who embrace the brutality of sharia so enthusiastically you get the impression they enjoy seeing people mutilated and murdered and their religion is just a convenient excuse; scripture-sodden oafs who seem to compete with each other to see who can issue the most fatuous fatwa degrading and humiliating women as much as possible.

Recently, for example, one Saudi "scholar" declared that women could associate with men they aren't related to by breast-feeding them, which would technically make them their sons.

Resourceful, or round the twist? Answers on a postcard to the king of Saudi Arabia. Another Saudi "scholar" is on record as saying women should have to cover themselves so completely that only one eye is visible. What, a whole eye? How shameless. Well, that's the modern world for you.

No doubt he would agree with the Iranian "scholar" who earlier this year made the extraordinary statement that immodestly dressed women are the cause of earthquakes, no less.

Some of these guys really do have a very serious problem with women, don't they? It's way beyond anything you'd call a simple neurosis and deep into hardcore mental illness. It's a shame that Allah, for all his omnipotence, doesn't seem to know any good psychiatrists.

If the Saudis couldn't dig money straight out of the ground they'd still be living in the Stone Age, as would the entire Arab world, which has produced absolutely nothing of value to humanity for centuries, thanks to a suffocating religion that fosters insularity and ignorance, not to mention a chronic and crippling sexual repression that makes Catholicism look like San Francisco in the 1960s.

And the damage this does can be seen in many places in the Islamic world, not least in the country of Pakistan, which is not, strictly speaking, an Islamic dictatorship, but it might as well be. It's a democracy, a fragile and corrupt democracy with nuclear weapons. Great. It's also a very Islamic country. How Islamic? Blasphemy carries the death penalty, and it doesn't get any more Islamic than that.

Indeed, right at this moment a woman is awaiting death by hanging because she happened to get into an argument with some Muslims who promptly accused her of blasphemy. That's how Islamic Pakistan is.

In fact, it's such an Islamic country that eighty percent of Pakistani women are regularly beaten by their husbands, and in the area around the city of Karachi a woman is murdered every day.

However, the Pakistani government is less concerned about these cowardly atrocities than it is about religious offence, taking care to block websites critical of Islam because they don't want anyone's morals corrupted. Meanwhile, Pakistan distinguishes itself on the internet by leading the world in Google searches for animal sex, child sex and rape sex. Normal consensual sex between human adults is apparently something of a minority taste in that devout country, according to Google.

Given all this, you might be surprised to hear that both Pakistan and Saudi Arabia have recently been appointed to the board of the new United Nations agency for women.

Yes, that's right, I said women. Both of these countries will be doing all they can to work for the empowerment and equality of women all over the world. Isn't that great news?

And how wonderfully inclusive of the United Nations to hand the fox the keys to the hen house yet again.

Yes, OK, these countries may well treat women like dogs, but hey, that's their culture, right? And we've got to respect it, don't we? Who are we to judge, after all? It's all just relative, anyway, isn't it? Just because a thing is insane and barbaric and downright evil, does that necessarily make it wrong? Surely we're not arrogant enough to assume that our values are superior just because they're more civilised, or that their values are somehow less valid just because we've got stringent laws against them? That would be disrespectful, and most intolerant, and quite probably racist.

No, in the spirit of mutual understanding and tolerance and respect and harmony and bridge-building, and all the other bullshit buzzwords of the new PC totalitarianism, we simply have to accept that brutalising half of humanity for the sake of pathetically inadequate male egos and primitive superstition is just part of the rich tapestry, the rich diversity, of cultures and faiths that so enrich us all. Isn't that right? Well, isn't it?

You know those bedbugs at the United Nations? I shouldn't worry too much about them. I think they'll leave of their own accord when they realise the company they're keeping.

80

Goodbye Sweden

December 1, 2010

This is a video I didn't want to make. No country in Europe has done more to embrace the multicultural nightmare... I mean dream... than Sweden (meaning no country has opened its arms wider to Muslim immigration) and these days every piece of news that comes out of Sweden is more and more disturbing.

Now we hear that the government there is so determined to dilute their culture clean out of existence they've actually changed the constitution without consulting the people.

You no longer have to be a Swedish citizen to hold sensitive or high government office (including national prosecutor, interestingly enough), and Swedes are constitutionally obliged to practise multiculturalism. In other words, it's now unconstitutional to uphold Swedish values in Sweden, because the people who run that country seem to think there's something intrinsically shameful or contemptible about being Swedish.

And I find this extremely puzzling, because all the Swedish people I've known have had every reason to be proud of who they are and of what their country is – or of what it was, and what it might be again one day if they ever come to their senses.

If anyone in Sweden is curious about the kind of image their country projects to the outside world, I ought to tell you that that image has changed considerably in recent years. Formerly regarded as one of the most pleasantly crime-free and civilised countries, Sweden is now officially the rape capital of Europe with twice as many rapes per capita as any other country, and twenty times more than some.

What do you suppose could have caused such a fundamental shift in the Swedish national character? It's the last place anyone would have expected an epidemic of rape.

It can't have anything to do with immigrant Islamic culture, of course, because nothing bad ever does. (That's the culture that teaches young men that women who are not covered from head to toe are asking to be raped – yes, that's the one.)

So realistically there can be only one explanation for anyone who isn't prejudiced and racist. And that is that Swedish men must have something very seriously wrong with them. Maybe they should seek psychiatric help. Seriously, guys, you need it.

You won't hear very much about immigrant rapists in Sweden because, for years, the government and press in that country have been conspiring in a crime against their own people to keep them in the dark, not only in winter, but in summer as well.

Swedish newspapers are heavily subsidised with government money, so journalists routinely censor the news to ensure that immigrants are never portrayed in a bad light and non-Swedish criminals are never identified as such, and this creates the cosy illusion that there are no immigrant rapists in Sweden. And this is very odd because next door in Norway that's pretty much all they've got.

According to the Oslo police, all the aggravated rapes in that city over a recent three-year period, all forty-one of them, were committed by immigrants from the Middle East and Africa and were characterised by gross violence.

That's bad news for Norwegian women, but if you live in Sweden you don't need to worry because there are no immigrant rapists in Sweden. Just ask any journalist.

For those of us watching from outside, especially after recent events, it's hard not to conclude that we're witnessing the open theft of an entire country, and all we can do is watch in astonishment and horror.

If I was a bookmaker I would no longer be taking bets as to whether Sweden becomes the first European Islamic state, because now it's only a matter of time.

And if anyone still doubts that this multicultural lie is anything other than a euphemism for deliberate Islamisation, you might like to know that despite Sweden's ravenous appetite for Muslims, more Muslims and yet more Muslims, no country has deported more Iraqi Christians back to Iraq to be butchered like Christmas turkeys for the crime of not being Muslims, because in Sweden it seems only Muslims are entitled to full human rights.

You won't be surprised to hear that Sweden is also a leading light in the new politically correct anti-Semitism we're seeing in Europe, and Jews no longer feel safe living there. Congratulations, Sweden. That's quite a double. Rape and anti-Semitism. You're carving out a real reputation for yourselves up there in the land of the midnight sun – or should that be the crescent moon?

When it was reported earlier this year that Jews who have lived in the city of Malmo for generations are being driven out by, guess who, Muslim immigrants, the mayor of that city washed his hands of the matter with an equanimity worthy of Pontius Pilate, even stooping so low as to blame the Israeli government for his own moral cowardice. He said Jews in Sweden should distance themselves from Israel's actions if they want to avoid being abused. And that seems to be how things work in Sweden nowadays. To avoid offending the criminal it's easier to blame the victim, and, in this case, adopt the Muslim terrorist position that every Jew is a foot soldier for Israel.

One inconvenient fact, however, is that the Koran tells Muslims to hate Jews because they're Jews, not because of Palestine. It doesn't mention the Palestinians. And if Israel disappeared tomorrow Jews in Sweden, and all over Europe, would still be harassed and abused by ignorant hate-filled Muslim immigrants for being Jews and for no other reason. And then all you multicultural dhimmis-in-waiting would have to find another mealy-mouthed excuse to look the other way.

Fortunately for Jews, they've had a lot of practice at taking abuse and they've got fairly broad shoulders which, of course, they need to carry around all those Nobel Prizes. Statistically a Jew is thousands of times more likely than a Muslim to win a Nobel Prize, and there can be only one reason for that, can't there? That's right, Islamophobia.

Clearly, the Nobel committees have an irrational prejudice against religion-induced ignorance, and they're obviously in need of some urgent cultural awareness and sensitivity training.

Maybe the Swedish government could step in and take a

moral stand; expel the Nobel Prize from the country and tell it to relocate to Tel Aviv where it belongs.

Admittedly, they would disgrace themselves and debase their country and embarrass the entire free world if they did so, but they're doing that already, so what's the difference?

81

Your Faith Is a Joke

December 16, 2010

If you criticise religion, every so often somebody will say to you quite disapprovingly: "You may not have faith in God, but you could show a bit more respect for those people who do."

And you might find yourself thinking: Actually, maybe they're right. It wouldn't hurt to show a bit more respect. After all, nobody likes to be told point blank that their religion is a crock of delusional garbage and a force for evil in the world, that what they call faith is merely fear dressed up as virtue, and that their puerile beliefs are a straitjacket on the whole of humanity. That's bound to put anybody's nose out of joint.

So yes, maybe I could show a bit more respect. The only fly in the ointment is I don't actually feel any respect. I have tried, I really have, and I feel terrible about it, but it just isn't there.

I suppose I could lie to myself and pretend for the sake of people's feelings (we all know how delicate and tender they can be these days) but the bald truth is I don't actually care about their feelings at all, not even slightly. And of course I realise this should weigh heavily on my conscience, but luckily my conscience knows when it's being bullied and manipulated, so it doesn't care either.

My conscience knows that there is no earthly reason for anybody on this planet to respect religion in any way. Indeed, purely on the evidence religion itself provides in such regular abundance, there's every reason to actively disrespect it to the point of outright abuse. And, quite frankly, the fact that religion gets so little abuse compared to what it really deserves I can only attribute to the unbelievable tolerance, restraint and plain good manners of atheists and secularists everywhere.

So, if you are a religious person, and if you're thinking about demanding more respect for your beliefs, please try to bear in mind that you and your religion are already getting way more respect than you have ever deserved. Your faith is a joke. Your god is a joke. He's so absurd he's an embarrassment even to people who don't believe in him, and he and you still have it all to prove. So far, no proof has been forthcoming, nor is it likely to be, as we all well know. So respect, I'm afraid, is out of the question. The best you can hope for is amused incredulity, and that would be on a good day.

People say you can only truly understand faith when you have faith, which I take to mean when you've suspended your critical faculties and hypnotised yourself into believing a load of fascist nonsense about your eternal soul, then you'll understand faith. I can certainly believe that.

Faith-peddlers like to put themselves beyond question by claiming their faith transcends reason, the very thing that calls it to account. How convenient.

Yes, faith transcends reason the way a criminal transcends the law. The word "transcendent" is very popular with religious hustlers because they never have to explain precisely what they mean by it, other than some vague superior state of understanding more profound than mere reason, which is crude and simplistic next to the subtleties and profundities of belief without evidence.

If you hear a senior clergyman (and you will) using the word "transcendent" to explain the nonsense he claims to believe, then you know two things: One, he doesn't know what he's talking about; and two, he doesn't want you to know what he's talking about either.

Faith doesn't transcend reason at all. Faith side-steps reason. It runs away from reason because reason threatens its cosy bubble of delusion; so faith disqualifies reason the way a Dutch criminal court disqualifies truth and witnesses, and for much the same reason.

If you're a believer, your faith allows you to adopt a set of beliefs that make absolutely no sense, knowing you won't be measured by whether they make sense, but by the level of piety you exhibit in believing them. In other words, your willingness to deny reality becomes a measure of your virtue. No wonder religion is so popular.

But what a price you pay for this virtue. You've been persuaded that believing the impossible is your only hope (how did that happen?) and that your purpose is to worship something beyond your understanding, defined by, and only accessible through, self-appointed intermediaries.

Your thoughts, your words and your identity are no longer

solely yours to decide, but are subject to the approval of those who have assumed authority over you through your faith; the people who have told you that you were born with something wrong with you (come on!), in a state of sin, no less, a condition that can only be cured by complete submission and obedience to them (surprise surprise) from the moment you're born to the moment you die.

And if all this doesn't exactly flatter your ego (and why should it?) don't worry, we can give it a special name to make you feel better and persuade you that you've still got some dignity. Let's call it faith, and let's deem it to be the highest and most noble and profound of all virtues. And let's pretend that it comes from within, when we all know that nothing about your religion is allowed to come from within because that would give you strength and freedom, the two things your religion wants as far away from you as possible.

Faith is the grip that clergy have over you. It's the invisible rope around your neck that pulls you along the road they want you to travel, for their benefit, not yours.

It's a dead-end word. It's a word of bondage. It's a word that lets you believe what you've been told to believe without feeling that you've been told what to believe, but you have, and you can stop pretending any time you like.

It's not a virtue; that's the last thing it is. It's an abdication from reality. It's a dumb act of self-hypnosis. It's a cowardly cop out. It's gullibility with a halo, and hiding behind it is like pretending to be an invalid.

So I don't really understand exactly what it is that I'm supposed to respect. It seems to me I'd need to be some kind of moral contortionist to respect something that noxious; something that depends for its existence on a closed mind, and that's clearly dragging humanity in the wrong direction and giving us false ideas about ourselves and about the nature of reality.

I feel if I respected that I'd be needlessly contributing to the stupidity and ignorance of the human race, and that's one thing I don't want on my conscience. No offence.

82

Godless Christmas

December 22, 2010

If you're an atheist, one question will crop up with predictable regularity at this time of year, and that is: "Why do you celebrate Christmas?"

Well, I can't speak for other atheists, but I celebrate Christmas not because it's a Christian festival, which it isn't, and not because it's a pagan festival, which it is if it's anything, but simply because it's a great excuse to celebrate something and drink a few beers in the dark days of midwinter. If Christmas didn't exist I would personally invent it for that very reason.

Of course I'm not crazy about the phoney Christian mask it's forced to wear, but that won't last forever, and, in the meantime, if there's any chance that it will offend some loudmouthed Islamist toerag or some self-hating multicultural PC thumbsucker, then I'm more than happy to celebrate it with all the bells and whistles I can muster, Baby Jesus and all.

So you could say that I celebrate Christmas, at least in part, for religious reasons, and I never thought I'd hear myself say those words.

Well, all right then, cultural reasons, but these days it's so hard to tell the difference, isn't it?

Having said all that, I do have to wonder why Christianity is allowed to hog the whole religious cake at Christmas. What happened to diversity and mutual understanding and cultural awareness and respect and bridge-building and blah blah etcetera etcetera? Don't tell me these are all just empty buzzwords.

Surely somebody has to get the ball rolling here, so I've decided that this year I'll be having an Islamic-themed Christmas, although I'll call it a multicultural Christmas so that nobody gets too alarmed.

Besides, between you and me, I heard a rumour that Santa Claus has converted to Islam and everyone's getting a fatwa in their Christmas stocking. I don't know how true it is, but frankly the last thing I need is to get on the wrong side of an Islamic Santa Claus. (You know what these converts can be like.)

So, although I will be getting in some beer, obviously (because Christmas without beer is like Eid without blood – it just wouldn't work), I'll try to make up for it in other more Islamic ways. I'll see if I can find a homosexual-looking angel for the top of the tree that we can all stone to death when we've had a few. And I'll try and get hold of some of those Islamic balloons I heard about that blow themselves up. It should be quite a party.

If we decide to play a traditional Christmas board game, say Trivial Pursuit or something like that, it goes without saying that a woman's answer will be worth only half that of a man. Not that it will really matter, because the women will have their own separate game in a smaller room in a less comfortable part of the house, while the men sit around stroking their beards and congratulating each other on how important they are. What a wonderful harmonisation of cultures.

Of course Christmas is not just about celebration and frivolity, it's also a time for reflection, which doesn't mean wearing mirrored sunglasses, no. It means thinking about stuff. (Unless that's against your religion, in which case I'd probably go with the sunglasses.)

This year I'll be taking time to spare a thought for those less fortunate, which would include all those poor long-faced Islamists over at the Muslim Council of Britain. There'll be no alcohol for them this Christmas, poor sods. Well, not in public, anyway, eh lads?

The same goes for the suit-and-tie jihadis at the Hamas front group hilariously known as the Council on American-Islamic Relations. As it's the season of goodwill, I thought about sending both of these groups a little gift token for some Gillette products so they could tidy themselves up for the holiday season, but then I thought they might take it the wrong way, and I didn't want to cause offence because that would make me a racist, and nobody wants to be a racist at Christmas! What would Little Baby Jesus think?

So instead I'll settle for a simple friendly greeting and say: Merry Christmas, boys. I wish you all the very best of mental health. In other words, get well soon.

To everybody else, I'd like to say that Christmas is a cultural festival that is a long-standing tradition in the western world, and I think it should be actively preserved and actively asserted for cultural reasons, because we all know how important they are.

I don't think it matters that Christians insist it's all about Little Baby Jesus, because I think most people realise that Christianity imposed itself on an older religion by hijacking its festivals, changing their names, and assiduously persecuting its followers, and that, frankly, Christianity's claim on Christmas is nothing less than an affront to human decency, but because it's Christmas and we're all in such a good mood we don't really care.

Personally, I think it's a good idea to celebrate the solstice, because we know it's actually real. And, of course, it reminds us of the greater reality that this planet is flying through space in an annual orbit around the sun, itself just a star among billions of stars in orbit around the black hole at the centre of our galaxy, itself part of a cluster of galaxies; and that some time in the future, our galaxy will collide with the Andromeda galaxy which is presently hurtling towards us at a quarter of a million miles an hour. And there's nothing that God or Allah or Little Baby Jesus or anybody else can do about that, no matter how many times we prostrate ourselves or how many prayers we offer from now until it does happen, about five billion years down the line.

And that's only if our sun hasn't already swollen up to a red giant by then and incinerated the entire inner solar system, along with God, Allah, Little Baby Jesus and all the other assorted pantomime characters of the human imagination, which itself will no longer even be a memory. Oh well. Easy come, easy go. Peace, and merry Christmas.

83

American Islamophobia

January 11, 2011

What happens in America matters to the entire free world, and these days America, like most places, is infested with Islamic supremacist pressure groups who falsely claim to speak for all Muslims, and who spend their time playing the professional victim, pestering politicians and law enforcement agencies with their constant whining and complaining and bellyaching and bitching and demanding special treatment.

One of these groups, the ludicrously named Council on American-Islamic Relations, has been quite busy recently setting up a new department dedicated to guess what – Islamophobia. Who would have predicted that?

They'll be looking for Islamophobia everywhere in America, and you know they're going to find it because they see it everywhere. My bet is it's only a matter of time before they contrive to find it right in the Oval Office. Obama's already on one knee to Islam. It shouldn't take much to get him down on two.

Islamophobia is a word that says a lot more about the person using it than the one it's directed at, so if you're ever tempted to throw it at somebody, try to bear that in mind. When I hear the word I know I'm listening to someone whose intelligence and judgment have been corrupted by the cultural Marxism of political correctness, and whose opinions need no longer be taken seriously.

What amazes me is that anyone takes this phoney word seriously. Young people can be forgiven for thinking it has always been part of the language, but this word didn't exist just a few years ago. It was deliberately invented by Islamic supremacists and their left-wing enablers as a way to silence critics of Islamic brutality, intolerance, misogyny, homophobia and anti-Semitism, and to stigmatise those who oppose religious fascism by inferring that they have a mental disorder.

Of course, there are only so many times you can tell someone who doesn't want to hear it that a phobia is an irrational fear and there's nothing remotely irrational about fearing Islam, especially if you happen to be female or gay or Jewish – or all three.

What is irrational is indulging Islam and pretending it's just another religion. That's more than irrational. It's downright stupid. It's as foolish as keeping a large predatory wild animal as a pet. Sooner or later you will be eaten, and you will deserve it.

People who oppose Islam are not Islamophobic. They're Islamo-realistic. They've had years of abundant and consistent evidence, and they see the religion for what it is – a supremacist totalitarian ideology using its peaceful followers as a shield to exploit religious freedom for political ends.

And Islamophobia is part of the scam, but Islamophobia doesn't exist, especially not in America, and recent figures prove it. According to the FBI there are ten times more hate crimes against Jews and gays in America than there are against Muslims. And the same thing applies in figures compiled by individual states – California, New York: way more crimes against Jews and gays.

How unfortunate for the Islamofascists that these cold hard facts should emerge just as they've set up their shiny new department dedicated to finding evidence of this mythical crime. Do you think these liars will now shut down this department and apologise for lying, or do you think they'll carry on lying, complaining, whining, bellyaching, bitching and demanding special treatment? Tough call, isn't it? I guess we'll just have to wait and see.

It must be quite galling for these guys to know that, although people may resent Islam (and who can blame them for that?) they don't resent Muslims, as two young Muslim men found out a few months ago when they drove thirteen thousand miles around America and were welcomed wherever they went.

The biggest hate crime against Muslims in America is the existence of the Council on American-Islamic Relations. If you're a Muslim American who wants to live in peace and freedom (and presumably that's why you're in America in the first place) these people are your worst enemy. They're parasites on your identity. They don't represent you. They claim ownership of you. Everything they do and say reflects back badly on you, yet you are the only thing giving them a veneer of respectability. Without you, these fanatics would be standing on street corners shouting at people.

They push the phoney lie of Islamophobia in order to marginalise and ghettoise you, to make you feel like a victim, because their whole existence depends on you being a victim.

They claim to challenge stereotyping of Muslims, and how do they do it? By stereotyping Muslims as professional complainers and malcontents who always want special treatment, who can't take the slightest criticism, and who are aggressively litigious to the point of obsession.

These people are the problem. They're not the solution. If they could, they would rule you with a rod of iron. You know they want to impose sharia – everybody does. And you also know, if you've got any sense, that no Muslim in the United States would be better off under sharia. So I have to ask you why you let them go on national TV time and time and time again claiming to speak for you, and why you let the TV networks get away with treating them as if they do.

The Council on American-Islamic Relations have had a lot of mileage out of their phoney-baloney Islamophobia. It must be quite devastating for them to be confronted with concrete proof that this thing is entirely imaginary when they've staked so much on it. It must be like the Pope finding out there's no Holy Ghost.

Now, if you insist on believing in Islamophobia you'll have to do so despite the evidence. You'll have to accept it on faith. As Mark Twain might have put it, you'll have to believe what you know ain't so.

Islamophobia ain't so. And you know it.

The Islamofascists have done their very best to talk it into existence and to wish it into existence, but, try as they might, they just can't persuade Americans to hate Muslims. Isn't reality a bitch?

84

The Criminal Truth

January 28, 2011

If you criticise the religion of peace you're likely to be accused of hate speech by people who will go on to abuse and threaten you as graphically and disgustingly as their fevered imaginations will allow, yet you'll be the one guilty of hate speech.

And if you're unlucky enough to live in certain parts of Europe you will also be prosecuted as a criminal.

Anyone who thought Denmark's experience with the cartoons might encourage that country to grow a backbone will be dismayed to hear that Denmark is the latest European country to persecute its own citizens for telling the truth about the religion of permanent offence.

This week Lars Hedegaard, president of the Free Press Society, is on trial in Denmark for accurately referring to the comparatively high number of family rapes in Islamic culture.

As most people know, violence against women and girls is one of the things that make Islamic culture distinctly inferior to western culture. Not different, but significantly less civilised.

However, the Danish authorities would like people to pretend that Islamic violence against women and girls doesn't exist, because otherwise they might have to do something about it, and that's the last thing they want, because that would mean rioting in the streets and barricades and burning cars and all the rest of it, and Danish people travelling in Muslim countries might also be attacked and killed. So they'd rather pretend it isn't happening and criminalise anyone who says it is. It's much safer for them to victimise their own people because they know there won't be any rioting and nobody will be murdered.

In this trial, as with the other two show trials currently under way in the Netherlands and Austria, the truth is no defence, because this is not about establishing the truth or upholding the truth (which is what justice is supposed to do). It's about suppressing the truth to appease the threat of Muslim violence, which makes it an act of cultural terrorism. And it's compounded by the fact that we haven't heard a word about any of this from the western media, the so-called free press, who seem to want to keep it as their little secret. If not for the internet, nobody would even know this trial was happening, or the one in Austria for that matter.

Causing offence is now a crime in several European countries. Doesn't anyone in the western media have anything critical to say about that at all? Or are they too stupid and complacent to realise that these laws also threaten the freedom of the press, as well as that of ordinary people to express an honest opinion?

One of the most pernicious lies of our time is the lie that all cultures are equal, when they're clearly, visibly, provably not even close to being equal. They're barely on the same planet is how unequal they are. But we walk on eggshells over this in the West because we're so riddled with post-imperialist guilt, which for some reason we've decided to regard as a chastening virtue and not as a crippling curse.

When you allow millions of people to immigrate from places where they mutilate their daughters as a matter of course, where they kill them in a heartbeat over some twisted sense of honour, and where rape victims are treated as criminals, it doesn't take a genius to know that you're going to be importing these values and attitudes as well, wholesale, unless you take steps to prevent it. And that is something we have spectacularly failed to do in Europe. Indeed, we've encouraged it by fostering separatism and ghettoisation in the guise of our old friend multiculturalism. As a consequence, Islamic violence against women and girls is an ugly reality in Europe. And for anyone to use the law to try to suppress discussion of it is not enlightened or tolerant or liberal. It's shameful and stupid and cowardly and unforgivable. It's cultural pollution at a criminal level. And if you live in Europe, your grandchildren will pay the price, and they'll despise you and everyone else alive today for letting it happen.

Our civilisation was fused in the crucible of opposing ideas freely expressed. That's the magic secret. It's the gold standard that has made us what we are, and made our society the most advanced in human history. And we have an obligation to uphold that standard, no matter what, for the sake of future generations. Despite the avalanche of rights we've been showered with in recent years, ducking out of this is one right we don't have, because without the right to speak your mind, all other rights are worthless.

Free speech is not the property of this generation of spineless appeasers. It's as intrinsic and essential a part of our identity as the Koran is for Muslims, and nobody has the right to restrict it or to modify it, regardless of who claims to be offended.

Anyone who insists on being offended is welcome to grow a thicker skin or go and live somewhere else. And if they don't like that they can go to hell – and that includes all public prosecutors, and the horse they rode in on.

85

The Taste of Multiculturalism

February 11, 2011

This week in Britain the multicultural left have had their knickers in a twist because the prime minister dared to criticise their sacred ideology. In fact, he did more than criticise it; he condemned it outright as a failure, and about time too.

However, I think he let them off rather lightly, given the actual scale of the crime, so allow me to add a few further notes to Mr Cameron's remarks.

Multiculturalism would be a good thing if it was what it pretends to be, which is a society where everyone is equally respected and mutually enriched. What could be better?

In practice, however, it means everybody has to focus on Islam. It means everybody has to worry about what Islam might think about this or that aspect of life and adjust their perspective accordingly, never the other way round. Have you noticed?

And this is a problem we have with a whole host of very positive sounding words that have become multicultural words in that they no longer mean what they say. These words now have a sugar coating and a poison centre.

Diversity, for example. Who could fail to be enriched by genuine diversity? In practice, however, diversity means everybody has to focus on Islam. It means everybody has to worry about what Islam might think about this or that aspect of life and adjust their perspective accordingly, never the other way round.

Tolerance is another word with a rosy multicultural glow about it (even if those who like to wallow in the language of tolerance are often the least likely to exhibit any). And this is because tolerance means everybody has to focus on Islam. It means everybody has to worry about what Islam might think about this or that aspect of life – and it's the same story right the way down the list.

Respect? Everybody focus on Islam. Community cohesion? Islam again. Bridge-building, mutual understanding? Everybody focus on you know who. Cultural awareness? You've guessed it.

Would you like a crash course now in cultural awareness? Here it comes. Islam should get whatever it demands. All criticism of it is racism. That's it. You are now as culturally aware as you will ever need to be. Isn't that reassuring?

The word "multiculturalism" only exists because of the religion of peace. It was invented to cushion the fact that Islam dominates – it doesn't integrate. We've had different cultures living side by side in Britain for years before this religion came along, but it was only then that they had to coin this euphemism to hide the unpleasant truth, and to soften us up for the inevitable incessant demands for separate standards and special treatment. Some people call it stealth jihad, and if you'd like to see an example of it up close and personal, just check your dinner plate.

If you live in Britain and if you eat meat, you're eating the barbarism of halal without being told about it. It's everywhere now – supermarkets, hospitals, schools, sporting venues – you can't get away from it even if you want to.

Halal is a guarantee that the animal you're eating died slowly in pain and terror, choking on its own blood – because you won't be surprised to hear that Islam's treatment of animals is every bit as brutal and disgusting as its treatment of human beings.

Religious slaughter violates our laws on animal cruelty in Britain, but we allow it because Muslims (and Jews, for that matter) insist on behaving as if it's still the Bronze Age, effectively torturing animals to death for the sake of their primitive superstitions. You can bet your life that if Christians engaged in this kind of self-indulgent cruelty it would have been stamped out a long time ago.

As it's not economically viable to process this meat separately, and as there can be no compromise with Islam (because that might cause offence – heaven forbid!), it goes without saying that everybody has to do it the Muslim way.

Supermarkets are refusing to label this stuff. They don't want people to know what they're buying, because they know that if they did they wouldn't buy it. And the government, Mr Cameron's government, is letting them get away with this.

And it means that if you live in multicultural Britain you are having Islam literally shoved down your throat. How does it taste? Does it taste like peace?

86

Andy Choudary Rides Again

February 28, 2011

I hear that Andy Choudary, Britain's favourite hate-preaching Islamist buffoon, intends to demonstrate outside the White House for the establishment of sharia in America.

I was wondering when we would hear from this arsehole again. Every year, it seems, about this time he gets himself into the media by promising some ridiculous stunt or other, and this seems to be the latest.

Given his record, there's no guarantee that Andy Choudary will even be allowed into America, which is, I suspect, what he's hoping – that they'll deny him entry and he can denounce them as hypocrites.

So please let him in, America. Try to overlook his support for 9/11 and give this windbag all the air time he wants on TV. I promise he'll entertain and infuriate. Frankly, I'm surprised Fox News haven't already got him under contract, because he's guaranteed to keep everyone's blood pressure nicely bubbling.

Let him tell you how much he hates America, how Americans

are the world's greatest criminals, and how the flag of Islam will fly over the White House. (Some would argue that it's already halfway up the flagpole under this administration.) And make sure you call him Andy. He absolutely hates that, because it reminds him of who he really is – a middle-class Pakistani boy from Welling with too much time on his hands. And just for the record, he's not an imam or any kind of authority on anything except scrounging benefit money from the state he claims to despise. He's just a guy off the street with a big mouth and mental problems who has managed to gather a little gang of like-minded casualties around him, and he represents nobody but himself and his little group of hysterical swivel-eyed bearded muppets.

Here in Britain, Andy Choudary long ago transcended the status of mere laughing stock, thanks to a tabloid press that glee-fully gives him all the coverage he wants, mainly because it's easier than journalism.

Indeed, in Britain he's now regarded as such an absurd oaf that we often wonder why his fellow fanatics allow him to be their spokesman at all, given the level of ridicule he attracts and will always attract. They may be insane, these guys, but they can't all be stupid. Some of them must be wondering: "How come this fat bastard gets all the attention, and not me? I'm a better Muslim than he is. I didn't spend my youth drinking, tak-ing drugs and chasing women. And I certainly wouldn't draw the level of ridicule he does. Nobody would. Yet his fat face is in the media all the time. He's being allowed to turn this into a personality cult, and he's making fools of all of us." And they'd be right, for once in their lives.

Yes, Andy Choudary is undoubtedly a joke. But his message is no joke. His message is pure evil. It's anti-human, and, if you believe in God, it's anti-God. He isn't just the poison face of Islam, this guy, but the poison face of humanity, and he's a prime walking example of the damage religion can do to the human mind.

To be fair to him, his fanaticism doesn't allow for subtlety, so, unlike the stealth jihadis, he doesn't engage in *taqiyya*, saying one thing while meaning another. There's no talk of harmony or tolerance or community cohesion. He tells it like it is. You submit to Islam. End of story.

He's honest enough to make it clear that Islam is not a religion of peace, but of submission. And there are no halfway measures, no small print, no get-out clauses. You submit to a religion that steps on your neck five times every day, and, if you decide that's not quite to your taste and change your mind, the penalty is death. Any takers?

Of course, if you're gay, the penalty is death anyway, and all that needs to be determined is whether you should be stoned or thrown from the top of a mountain. One for the scholars there.

The Muslim Brotherhood front groups who claim to speak for all Muslims in the West are embarrassed by Andy Choudary, because his manifesto is exactly identical to theirs, only Andy lays it bare for all to see, which is not what they want – at this stage.

They'd rather stick to the fictional narrative of tolerance and harmony and respect that has already sucked in so many gullible lawmakers, but Andy, bless his big mouth, just keeps giving the game away.

So please let him in, America. You'll be doing yourselves and everybody else a big favour if you do. Let him take his little gang of fuzzy-faced freaks and social misfits to the White House, and let them demonstrate to their hearts' content, on live coast-to-coast TV if possible.

Let them call for sharia, with its brutal punishments, denial of rights for women, death for gays and the whole grim catalogue of barbarism it represents, and let the American people be made fully aware of what the suit-and-tie jihadis would like to keep hidden, for the time being.

87

The Great Jesus Swindle

March 31, 2011

Spring has finally arrived here in the northern hemisphere, and at this time of year I tend to focus a lot more on the vegetable plot than on the internet, because I'd rather be outside in the open air than inside in front of a screen. However, you may take a different view. If so, this video is for you, especially if you're a Christian.

There are millions of people on this planet who claim to have a personal relationship with somebody called Jesus, yet each of those people, it seems, has a different Jesus in their imagination (which is where Jesus lives), a Jesus who shares all their particular values and prejudices. That's what he's there for, after all. It's how he earns his keep.

So if, for example, you don't like homosexuals very much, you can be sure your Jesus won't like them much either. It's really quite amazing. It's almost as if he can read your mind. But that's Jesus for you. There's nothing he can't do (except tolerate homosexuals, apparently).

As for abortion, don't even get him started on that subject. He's got plenty to say about abortion, although none of it actually appears in the Gospels. But don't you worry about that. He's dead against it if you are.

This is the beauty of Jesus. The magic, the miracle of Jesus, is that each of us can create him in our own image, and he can be whoever we want him to be. He's as versatile as Mr Potato Head. As for the man who it may have all been based on, if he ever existed, he's long gone – like Abraham Lincoln's famous axe that had both its head and handle replaced several times, yet was still as good as new.

I mention this because atheists also have their own version of Jesus – because Jesus, whether we like it or not, is a part of our culture. So yes, I have my version of Jesus even though I don't believe in God, and my Jesus despises Christianity as the greatest swindle ever perpetrated. Indeed, if my Jesus ever came face to face with a senior clergyman or a televangelist he'd be hard pressed not to slap him around the room and kick him down a flight of stairs.

There's a common misconception among Christians that the purpose of their religion is to spread the message of Jesus. In fact, the purpose of Christianity is to suppress the message of Jesus and to swindle you out of the kingdom of heaven.

Christianity is grounded in the notion that there is something fundamentally wrong with being born a human being. Original sin is possibly the most poisonous and self-destructive idea in human history, so naturally it has been enthusiastically embraced by clergy.

Whereas Jesus seeks to empower you, clergy seek to weaken

you, to make you feel small and helpless. They don't want you to consider the lilies of the field, or to seek the kingdom of heaven within, because that's too much like the message of Jesus.

They'd rather you focused instead on the ludicrous celestial psychodrama of God and Satan and angels and demons and hellfire, and burdened yourself with baseless guilt and morbid fear of eternal damnation.

They depict this earthly life as a grubby thing to be transcended, because they want you disconnected from the planet that gives you life, to feel that you're apart from nature, not a part of nature, because they don't want you grounded in any way. They want you rootless, uncertain, susceptible, while they hold out the promise of eternal salvation – access to the kingdom of heaven, no less – but only through them, as if they control the only bridge over the chasm of hellfire, and there's a toll to pay (of course there is) and the church bells ring: "Ker-ching! Ker-ching!"

They might as well be selling property on Jupiter. Yet they're legally allowed to get away with this fraud, and to pay no taxes on the vast proceeds. And that's why the Catholic Church today measures its wealth in tens of billions and if you live to be a thousand you'll never meet a poor televangelist.

Yet Jesus never asked anybody for money. Jesus never passed around a collection plate or got people to tithe part of their income to him. Everything he did, he did for free. He had lepers and cripples lining up around the block, and not one of them had medical insurance (can you believe the irresponsibility of those people?), but Jesus didn't care. He healed them anyway, absolutely free.

And when I say free, I don't mean free in a toll-free prayer line kind of way either, as in: "Call now, free, and there will be someone there to pray with you – and take your credit card number, so that by the time you hang up you'll be committed to making a regular monthly payment to somebody who flies around in a private jet." Not that kind of free.

In exploiting Jesus to swindle humanity, they've also managed to swindle Jesus. They've stolen his name and his identity and turned it into a commercial trademark. If he ever comes back he should sue.

Now Jesus is like Colonel Sanders. They're just using his picture. The difference is Colonel Sanders was bought out. Jesus has been sold out, and so have you, if you're a Christian. You've been framed for something you didn't do.

If Jesus really was crucified as per the Gospels, he didn't die for anybody's sins but his own. He died because he posed a threat to a group of people with strongly vested interests and very savage values. You may recall he told the Pharisees point blank where they could find the kingdom of heaven. Don't look here or there, he said, look within. But they didn't want to hear that any more than the modern Pharisees want to hear it, because they knew very well what he meant, that the kingdom of heaven is a state of awareness in the here and now that doesn't require the stewardship of professional clergy, and that if we took his advice to seek it within, not only would we find it, we'd find the strength and the wisdom to put them and their whole blood-sucking fear-mongering criminal racket permanently out of business. And because they lived in the kind of brutal society where they could have him put to death for his words, that's exactly what they did, just as they would today in certain Muslim countries.

But you don't have to feel guilty about it, because you weren't there. You had no opportunity to influence events. You are entirely blameless. And the only guilt that you need to feel is maybe a little passing sheepish embarrassment at ever having fallen for this insulting nonsense in the first place.

Anyway, that's enough from me. I'm going back outside now to consider the lilies of the field, and to plant a few potatoes in the good clean life-giving earth.

88

The Trouble with Christianity

April 14, 2011

I've had a number of strong responses to my last video from people who tell me I should be criticising Islam, not Christianity, because Islam is a major threat to our freedom. And yes, this is very true, but if not for the absurd level of respect, deference and privilege we accord religion in the West, Islam wouldn't be anywhere near the problem it is.

Besides, I think I may have mentioned Islam one or two times in the past, so I thought I'd take a break from the divisive Islamophobic racist hate-mongering to give my multicultural critics a chance to untwist their knickers and get their blood pressure down, while I pick on some weak and defenceless Christians purely for sport, because I guess that's the kind of person I am, and it's probably one of the reasons I'm going to hell – because apparently I am going to hell for rejecting Jesus, among other things. And I find this a puzzling accusation because if you watched the video you'll know that I don't reject Jesus. I reject religion. I'm happy to listen to Jesus all day long, as long as he keeps his mouth shut about religion. And specifically I reject Christianity, along with the clerical criminals who run Christianity, and the fake artificial Jesus they have invented for public consumption.

The man known as Saint Paul (for reasons I've never really understood) was the first one to push this supernatural nonsense about Jesus, but the early Church capitalised on it and exploited it enthusiastically. They needed Jesus to be a god so that they could use him to generate fear (which is the only level they know how to operate on) and also to claim supernatural authority through him, the best kind of authority to have when you're bluffing.

As a mere man, Jesus was almost useless to them. All he could offer were words of compassion and wisdom, and what earthly good would they be to the men who run the Church? That would be like handing a slide rule to a monkey.

So they needed to make him a god, but of course they already had a god, the same one they've got today, the fictional psychopath of the desert. So they had to find some way of conflating Jesus, author of the Sermon on the Mount, with this horrible monstrous entity of vengeance and death: quite a theological challenge that was always going to take some specialist bullshitting, but they finally managed it in the fourth century when they solidified the idea of the Trinity – the three gods in one, or the three-god trick, as I like to think of it. The classic Christian con – God the father, God the son and God the holy spirit; although if you're anything like me you might prefer the atheist trinity; that's God the imposter, God the fraud and God the wholly phoney – wholly as in entirely, completely and absolutely one hundred percent fake, false and phoney baloney, not to put too fine a point on it.

The Trinity is an outrageous piece of semantic flummery designed to confuse, not enlighten, and it follows a basic rule in religion, that ideally not only should the thing you believe in be absolutely impossible, but any explanation of it should be impossible to understand. And the Trinity obliges handsomely on both counts, as these three entities: the father (God), the son (Jesus), and the holy spirit (your guess is as good as mine) become as one, miraculously of course, while remaining separate, so that each is uniquely God yet each is completely God.

I know, you could listen to an explanation from now until next week and still be none the wiser, which is, of course, the whole idea.

We can argue about Jesus until we're blue in the face, about whether he existed and whether he was divine and all the rest of it, but some things are beyond dispute, and it is a matter of historical fact that the Trinity is pure invention by Christian clergy, so any Christian clergyman who tells you it's the truth is either ignorant of history or a goddamned liar.

Which do you think it is? Yeah, me too.

And this is what I reject. Not Jesus, but religion, and the clerical criminals who run it – the people who Jesus despised as much as I do. Whited sepulchres, he called them. Outwardly wholesome, inwardly rotten. And he was being way too kind in my opinion. And if I have to go to hell for my opinion (and it seems that I do), then so be it. I can think of worse things.

In fact, since I said in a previous video that I'd rather go to hell than be a Christian, I've been contacted by several people urging me to recant those foolish words and repent before it's too late. Hell is real, they tell me, Satan is real. And they say it with such conviction you just know they've got the information from some kind of infallible authority. Luckily, however, I'm quite looking forward to going to hell. I've heard so much about the place it almost seems like a home away from home to me now. I understand it's likely to be warmer than I'm used to, which surprises me, as life is warm and death is cold, so, if anything, you'd expect hell to be on the chilly side, but apparently it isn't, according the those who know.

I'm very grateful that so many experts have taken the trouble to testify to the definite existence of hell for my benefit. It's a real weight off my mind. I was beginning to worry that the idea of hell might be just a cynical ploy to intimidate weak-minded gullible people into submitting to religious fascism. How comforting to know it's real, and there really is everything to fear after death. Thank God for Satan. What would you Christians do without him?

So before we denigrate poor old Satan too much (I know he's everyone's favourite bad guy and everything, the lord of misrule and all that), but the next time you're down on your knees praying like an idiot you might want to think about offering a prayer of thanks to the big guy downstairs, because, without him in his essential role of universal bogeyman, none of this delusional nonsense of yours would even be possible. So in that sense, Satan is your saviour, not Jesus. What can I say? Them's the breaks.

89

Justice for Osama

May 8, 2011

I wasn't going to say anything about bin Laden's death. What is there to say, apart from good riddance? But the aftermath has become a lot more interesting than the event itself. Personally, I don't think the Americans did anything wrong, despite the noises we've been hearing all week, especially here in Europe, about legality and human rights and blah blah blah from people who would love to frame America as the bad guy here for taking out this enemy field commander and self-confessed mass murderer without allowing him access to an army of human rights lawyers eager to show he was suffering from low self-esteem and should be entitled to counselling and compensation.

The only people who should be apologising here are the Pakistanis – and they have said they're embarrassed, which makes a change. I was beginning to think nothing could embarrass that country.

They've had some questions to answer, which they have answered in the usual way, with excuses and lies and blaming everybody but themselves. I'm surprised they haven't demanded compensation. Oh, but wait, they already get three billion dollars a year from the American taxpayer, and another hefty chunk from the British taxpayer. The country is effectively living on welfare, but they can afford nuclear weapons. And despite being quite happy to take all this money, they've still shown that they simply can't be trusted. And that's why the Americans cut them out of the loop. It's a decision that would not have been taken lightly, but they knew damn well the Pakistanis would tip off bin Laden.

And these are the people we're trusting to keep the nuclear weapons out of the hands of terrorists. That's why the money is really being paid. It's protection, pure and simple. Pay up and nothing happens to the nukes. That way everybody's happy, and a few Pakistanis get very, very rich. (Or would that be a cynical assumption?)

Even now certain questions remain unanswered. Questions like: "Can the Pakistani intelligence service actually find their own arse in the dark with both hands, or can't they?" Given what has happened, I think they should have to physically prove it before that country gets any more money.

Meanwhile, President Obama deserves some credit for giving the go ahead to take out the trash, as it were, but, in truth, he needed this. He's a politician, and he needs to be popular. And he needs to show he's got a little Reagan in him as well, even if it is just for show, otherwise he knows he hasn't got a hope in hell of being re-elected.

He was careful to make the point that America is not at war with Islam, but he neglected to add that Islam is at war with

America, both from outside and inside the country. And talking of which, I'd like to know what kind of cultural awareness and sensitivity training the Navy SEALs received before being sent in. I hope they showed some respect and remembered to remove their shoes before entering. I also hope they didn't accidentally damage a copy of the Koran or, heaven forbid, interrupt anyone who was praying. I'd also like to know why local Muslim community leaders weren't consulted beforehand. That's bound to cause resentment and mistrust, which can sow the seeds of division.

I blame the Jews. Well, doesn't everybody?

They buried Osama at sea (or dumped him in the ocean, depending on your point of view) because they didn't want his grave to become a shrine. But they still gave him an Islamic funeral he didn't deserve as a goodwill gesture, which has been predictably taken as a slap in the face by the professional complainers in the Islamic world who wanted him buried in the ground facing Mecca and all done up with pretty bows.

One bearded buffoon even called it a declaration of war, but I don't know what kind of Rip van Winkle world he's been living in, because it seems to me that war was declared pretty unequivocally ten years ago when more than three thousand innocent people were murdered in the name of the religion of peace.

The Americans won't release photographs of the body because they say it might inflame things, but I'd say on balance flying planes into buildings is much more likely to inflame things, wouldn't you?

But what this means is that the conspiracy theories are now

in full flow. He isn't really dead. He was never even there. It's all as fake as the moon landings.

But it didn't have to be this way. They shouldn't need photographs to prove this guy is dead. They should have kept the body. They should have brought the son-of-a-bitch back to New York, pickled him in alcohol, and mounted him on top of the Ground Zero mosque with a pork chop in his mouth and a fireman's axe up his arse. (Or is that just me?) Facing Mecca, of course, because we wouldn't want to be disrespectful.

90

You'll Turn to God

May 13, 2011

When religious people realise they're not going to draw you into their fantasy world, they'll often say something like: "You wait. You'll turn to God when you're close to death."

It has an air of desperation about it, that statement, as well as considerable menace. You can almost hear the *Jaws* music in the background. "You'll turn to God when you're close to death" really means "You will submit – not because you want to, but because you're afraid not to."

Religion needs us to believe that death is something to be greatly feared without its protection, and the closer we get to it the greater the fear will become, until it builds to a crescendo of terror right at the final moment, and then, you better believe it, you'll turn to God, oh yes you will. So wouldn't it be easier to turn to God now and save yourself all that anguish?

Actually, when you put it like that it does sound like a tempting psychological refuge, but, I don't know what it is, I just can't seem to get past the fact that God doesn't exist.

"But what if you're wrong? What if he does exist? You don't know. What if hell exists? Wouldn't it be more prudent to take Pascal's Wager, and believe anyway just in case?"

Not really. Hell might well be very unpleasant, but the alternative to hell is far too horrible to contemplate. The alternative is submission. Real death. Death of the spirit, the thing religion feeds on and craves.

Pascal only makes his wager in the first place because he has been intimidated into it by the threat of eternal damnation, which I already embrace as the lesser of two evils, so I have no need for Pascal or his wretched wager.

Pascal says you might as well bet on God because you lose nothing and stand to gain everything, and it sounds attractive on the surface, but I reckon Pascal's bookie must have seen him coming, because the moment he places that wager he loses. He submits to religion, which is what religion wants him to do. And his motivation for doing so is pure naked fear.

Pascal has found a clever-dick way of rationalising it by calling it a wager, but in truth there is no wager. There is only craven capitulation under crude threat of punishment. Pascal is a clever man, a famous mathematician, but he might as well be an idiot, because he lets religion use its only weapon successfully against him. He knuckles under to fear. He caves in. He turns to God. He submits. And he's in with everything, because it's an all-or-nothing game, so, as we say in England, he's done his bollocks, he's done his rent. He loses.

The god of the desert is such a deeply unpleasant character I'd be ashamed and embarrassed to find myself turning to him, even after a few beers, for any reason other than to give him the finger – which is, by the way, what I do give anyone claiming to be his representative. He has no representatives. He doesn't exist. (I can't prove it, of course, but I have faith.)

He's so obviously manmade, this god, it's embarrassing. You can tell by the human limitations. Vengeful, narrow-minded, petty, ego-bound, quick to take offence, incredibly stupid – he's got our fingerprints all over him.

Look at the way he behaves the very first time we step out of line way back in Genesis. The entire race is permanently banished and a curse is put on all future generations. Even Gadaffi wouldn't go that far, would he? OK, maybe a bad example.

But am I the only one who thinks that's a gross overreaction on God's part, and a pretty obvious sign of insecurity? And if God is insecure he's not perfect. And if he's not perfect he's not God. So, even if he did exist, he'd be an imposter.

God reacts as he does in the Genesis fantasy because it's the only way he can react. He has nothing else in his locker. And that's because he was created by primitive superstitious desert-dwelling savages with no conception of civilisation or reality as we understand it. If they found themselves in the modern world they would die of fright. Yet we still allow them to impose from the grave their laughably narrow and ignorant world view on the whole of human civilisation. We must be insane.

The argument for religious faith would be an insult to an ape, let alone a human being. So why is religion popular? Because it's easy to explain to idiots. (Magic always is.) And, of course, to true believers – the third of the population, so it's reckoned, who have a need to believe, who want to believe, and who have taken a solemn vow of gullibility. And these are the people who, when push comes to shove, will warn you with comically grim foreboding that you'll turn to God when you're close to death.

But, if I were making a wager, I'd be inclined to bet that they will turn to God when they're close to death and find nobody there, except maybe old Pascal, religion's favourite mug punter, endlessly tearing up a betting slip. And these are the people who keep warning me about the horrors of hell. Well, you know what they say – you get what you focus on. Enjoy.

91

Come On, Ireland

May 20, 2011

OK, this is a video about politics, and here's a question: Should Ireland, long a province, be a nation once again? Whatever happened to that dream? It did flicker to life for a few decades, but those sunny days are now a distant memory because it's been snuffed out with ruthless Euro efficiency and today the president of Ireland is effectively an unelected Belgian.

This is because Ireland gave up its currency and joined the single European currency, which saddled the country with an artificially low interest rate, creating a massive bubble that has now burst spectacularly. And, because banks are more important than people, the government is bailing them out with massive amounts of the people's money borrowed at interest rates guaranteed to keep the next generation in poverty.

Understandably, people aren't very happy about this, so a couple of months ago they held an election in Ireland where they voted for a new future, which, as it turns out, is identical to the old future. Just because they called it an election doesn't mean it had anything to do with democratic self-determination. Ireland is a member the European Union where democracy means you can vote for anything you like as long as it's more of the same. So the Irish people were given a straight choice between more of the same and more of the same, but they couldn't make up their minds, so they've got a coalition of more of the same.

The European Union is very popular with politicians because it's very good to politicians; it was created for their benefit. It's not so good to voters, because it denies them a voice – another reason it's popular with politicians.

These days we in Europe no longer make most of our own laws. We have them handed down to us by people we haven't elected and can't remove. The people we do elect are powerless to change anything even if they wanted to, and most of them don't want to because they've got their snouts in the trough of a corrupt organisation whose accounts haven't been signed off by the auditors for the last sixteen years.

And we (the people, that is) haven't consented to any of this. We've had it steadily imposed upon us through duplicity and coercion, because in Europe today the grand project, political union, is more important than the people, and that's the bottom line. Nothing must ever be allowed to disrupt the project, especially not democracy. Indeed, if there's one thing a Euro politician despises and fears more than anything it's the democratic will of the people.

This is because many of those who run Europe today were politicised by sixties pseudo-Marxist utopianism, which they're still determined to impose on the people for their own good,

regardless of what the people might want. They believe in cen-
tralised state control, society as a project – their project. It's the
mentality that ran the old Soviet Union, and it's the mentality
that has driven the European Union forward against the wishes
of the European people, imposing a constitution on the whole
of Europe that hardly anyone was allowed to vote for, and
imposing a single currency on the whole of Europe that's falling apart at the seams. But they won't abandon it because they
consider it a vital step on the road to full political union and the
abolition of all European nation states under a central socialist
dictatorship.

So you can just imagine how inconvenient democracy is to
this mentality, when people have consistently shown they can't
be trusted to vote the way they're told. But what can they do?
They can't just abolish democracy, because that might raise
a few eyebrows, even in sleepy old Europe, so they practise a
kind of soft totalitarianism dressed up in the language of consensus that effectively neutralises democracy. Yes, you can vote
if you want to, but if you vote the wrong way you'll have to do
it again until you get it right, or your vote will be ignored, for
your own good.

Ireland was the only country in Europe that was allowed to
hold a referendum on the Lisbon Treaty, which establishes the
unwanted constitution for Europe. And that was only because
the Irish constitution insisted on a referendum, and their politicians couldn't weasel out of it the way they did everywhere else,
including Britain.

So we all watched the Irish referendum with great interest
because our future depended on the outcome. And when the

Irish people voted against the Lisbon Treaty we applauded them for it, and thanked our lucky stars for Irish democracy.

So what happened? Their vote was ignored and they were forced, by their own politicians, to vote again.

The second time they were bullied into voting in favour by a relentless, unanimous and heavily financed campaign of deliberate fear-mongering and lies by those same politicians, business leaders and the media, all desperate to sign away their country to all things Euro. And now look at Ireland, barely a province, let alone a nation, with massive unemployment and people once again leaving in droves. It's as if the last hundred years never happened. The Irish people have been conned into giving away their country. Their sovereignty has been swindled from them, and those responsible should be in jail. Once again they're finding out in Ireland the hard way that when other people control your destiny you cease to matter.

The Euro project is all that matters to the Euro fanatics, and if a few million people are reduced to poverty that's a price worth paying for ever closer union and ever more control. Thanks to the European Union, Ireland doesn't make its own laws or control its own borders – that's already a given – but now it doesn't even run its own economy. The country has been stripped and left shivering in its underwear. Yet the unelected president of the European Commission, Mr Barroso, unlike most of them not a closet Marxist, but a closet Maoist (I guess that's what they mean by diversity), had the nerve to blame the Irish people for their own misfortune, which is like slapping somebody with their own hand. It's what we call taking the piss.

But then Mr Barroso can afford to be so glibly dismissive. He's paid more than the American president, more than the British prime minister, so he's not feeling the squeeze, and he can't be removed by popular vote, so he doesn't have to give a damn.

If ever a man was asking for a political kick in the crotch it's this guy. And Ireland could be just the country to give it to him, because he and his cronies are now terrified that Ireland might just say enough is enough and withdraw from the single currency, and set an example to other countries that could bring their whole corrupt artificial house of cards crashing down; that Ireland could decide to stand on its own feet again, restore the punt, default on these oppressive predatory loans and tell the bankers and the Eurocrats to shove their extortionate interest rates right up their Lisbon Treaty. You know, like a nation once again.

But for that to happen, Ireland, you'll have to elect a leader, and not just another bloody politician. Good luck with that.

92

Let's Blame the Jews

May 26, 2011

In Europe today, one of the many unfortunate consequences of pandering to the bigotry of Muslim immigrants has been a rise in anti-Semitism – not that Europe has ever needed much encouragement on that score. And this has breathed life into a whole host of previously dormant conspiracy casualties who would love to believe that Jews control the world.

It seems like almost every day now I hear from somebody telling me that I should educate myself about Jews, how evil they are and how they manipulate everything so that they can control the world.

Apparently Jews are responsible for all kinds of horrible things, including 9/11 (that goes without saying) and even the curse of multiculturalism. That's right, all those Jews who are being driven out of Europe by hate-filled Muslim immigrants are actually victims of a Jewish plot to destabilise the world so that they can... control it, I guess. I don't know. I'm a little light on the details, but then most people are.

Compared to the number of Muslims and Christians on this planet, not to mention Hindus and Buddhists, Jews are a handful of people. They're a tiny percentage of the population. Nearly half of them live in Israel, a country the size of a county, and more are being driven there every day, especially from Europe, where it has become fashionable to use the Israeli government's behaviour as an excuse for the kind of open anti-Semitism we've become used to hearing from Muslims.

At anti-Israel demonstrations in Europe you're likely to hear calls for Jews to be gassed. We've even had the spectacle of a Dutch member of parliament in the front line of such an event.

In Sweden, Israeli athletes can no longer compete without being attacked by violent mobs, because the police can't or won't protect them.

Hate crimes against Jews outnumber those against Muslims, and many of them are carried out by Muslims, for no other reason than they've been taught from childhood to hate Jews. Meanwhile, day in and day out, we have to listen to their endless hypocritical horseshit about Islamophobia. It's enough to make you want to throw up.

I don't like some of the stuff the Israeli government does either, but I support Israel's right to exist and to defend itself against people prepared to use women and children as human shields.

I no longer believe the Israelis should give back Jerusalem. I still think they're holding it for a stupid reason (religion – it doesn't get any more stupid than that), but experience has taught us that the Islamic mentality views any concession as weakness to be exploited further; and besides, too many so-called Palestinians seem less concerned with peace and freedom than with driving the Jews into the sea, so the bombings wouldn't stop.

The whole world knows there could have been a peaceful settlement many times in the past but for incompetent and corrupt Palestinian leadership. Now in Gaza they've saddled themselves with Hamas, a bunch of fundamentalist religious thugs who don't want peace at any price.

For Hamas, the enemy is not Israel. The enemy is Jews. If you support Hamas you support people who want to exterminate Jews, not for being Israelis, but for being Jews, and you support a culture where Jew-hatred is bred right into the children. I hope you're proud of yourself.

I think Israel is in the wrong place – I've said it before. It couldn't be in a worse place, given the hateful mentality of its neighbours, but it's a bit late to do anything about that now.

The fact that a Jewish state needs to exist at all (and it does need to exist) is an indictment of all humanity, especially the Catholic Church, whose centuries-long programme of aggressive Jew hatred has been ingrained right into the European psyche, so that it takes almost nothing to bring it out.

And that's why, if I were a Jew, even a non-Zionist peace-campaigning liberal Jew (and there are plenty of them) I would want to see a strong Israel, because when push comes to shove, people will not stand up for Jews. We've seen it historically in Europe, and in the wake of the Muslim invasion, we're seeing it again today – especially from the self-styled anti-fascists. What a joke you people are.

The truth can often be painful when you don't want to hear it, but you're going to bloody well hear it anyway. And the truth is that Jews have contributed more to humanity than any other group of people. Way more than Muslims. Vastly more than Muslims. We're talking different-planet-more-than-Muslims.

Jews receive a disproportionate number of Nobel Prizes (real ones, I mean – not the bullshit peace one) because they're at the top of sciences, medicine, technology – you name it. Wherever there's progress in this world, you'll often find some Jew in there making all the difference.

Israel today is a world technological leader, alone in the Middle East, like a diamond in a sea of mud.

Compared to Jews, Muslims are passengers on planet earth getting a free ride. Even the wealth of the Muslim world comes pouring straight out of the ground. If it didn't, they wouldn't have any. It's pathetic, and it's no wonder the Muslim world is so quick to petulant childish anger. They must have a very poor self-image, and who can blame them?

But they're the only ones who can do anything about it. They can choose to drag themselves into the twenty-first century and leave this filthy garbage behind, or they can carry on humiliating and degrading themselves with hysterical Jew hatred, and we'll carry on judging them on it as an embarrassment to the human race. (I do hope that doesn't offend.)

As for you people who keep telling me that Jews control the world, even if that were true, I'd much rather that Jews control this world than Muslims any day, and so would every other sane person on the planet. But it isn't true, and I don't want to hear about it any more, if that wouldn't be too much trouble. So if you really believe that Jews are evil manipulators with their fingers in everyone's pie, or if you really believe that some sinister

Jewish cabal is controlling you from above like a marionette, then please don't tell me about it, tell a doctor – but maybe not a Jewish one.

93

Don't Pray for Me

June 10, 2011

One of the prices you pay for being godless is that people will keep threatening to pray for you, which can be a little creepy, as you know they're not praying for you to become happy and fulfilled, but for you to become religious, which is often far from the same thing. They're praying for their beliefs to have influence over your life. In other words, they're not praying for you at all, they're praying against you.

So, can I say to the people who have said they're praying for me, please don't do it. You're not doing any of us any good, and frankly you are wasting your time.

I'm beyond redemption. I categorically reject God and I wholeheartedly deny the holy spirit. I'm fully resigned to eternal damnation, and I'm absolutely fine with it. You'll be far better off praying for yourself because that's what you're doing anyway. And you never know, you might just get lucky, because I believe prayer, like religion itself, is all in the mind, which can be a very big place, in many cases.

We're very lucky that we live in an age when we know so much about the mind, apart from what it is, where it is, and how it works, obviously. We think it lives in the brain. Well, we're pretty sure it's there. The fact is we'd put money on it being there, but we can't be absolutely positive because, sadly, it's not yet possible to open the brain, cut out the mind, kill it, and display it in a glass case, but I'm sure that's just a matter of time, as science marches on.

One thing we do know about the mind is that it's extremely powerful and extremely malleable – not always an ideal combination. We know it's powerful enough to talk itself into just about anything, so that when religion comes along taking credit for the good stuff and making the bad stuff your fault, it becomes very easy to persuade yourself that you're an unworthy sinner, which is exactly what you'll become if you keep telling yourself that, because that's how the mind works. So you will be an unworthy sinner, but only because you talked yourself into it like an idiot. And now you've got to spend your whole life battling your own nature to remain virtuous. Is that stupid, or is it crazy? It's got to be one or the other.

Well, I've heard it said that prayer is also a kind of self-hypnosis. A way of programming the subconscious mind to work behind the scenes on your behalf. And in some ways that does make a lot of sense, because we know the body and mind are not, in fact, separate things.

We know that if you're thinking troublesome thoughts, for example, your muscles will tense up without you even realising it, and, if you keep it up, pretty soon different chemicals start getting produced until, before you know it, there's a whole different party going on in your body, just because of what you're thinking.

It's well known that optimistic people recover from illness more quickly than pessimists because their mind is working with them and for them, not against them.

So if you're praying for something, but you don't seem to be getting what you're praying for, maybe it's not because the supernatural has let you down, but because your subconscious mind believes that you don't deserve it. (And you thought God was judgmental.)

But where do you suppose your mind might have picked up an idea like that?

You see, this is why I think you'll be far more likely to pray successfully without religion than with it, because religion doesn't want you to feel you deserve it. Religion wants you to feel that you deserve to be on your knees in penitence and submission, praying for mercy. Religion wants life to be a fate worse than death. That's why it makes such a virtue of misery. To suffer is to be holy, right? You want to be like Jesus, don't you? Of course you do, otherwise how will you be saved from eternal torture? Compared to that fate, a little earthly suffering is actually a good investment. It's like money in the bank. And all it's going to cost you is a pair of sore knees and a crippling guilt complex. What a deal.

Seriously, pray for yourself. You're the one who needs it. And if you want to pray successfully for yourself, and I'm assuming that you do, then I'd suggest the first thing you need to do is dump religion, and then you need to convince yourself that you deserve it. You know you do, but you have to believe it, you have to have faith, otherwise you'll be wasting your time.

And I really hope it works out for you, but you don't have to worry about me. I'm calling religion's bluff, and I'm happily hurtling towards hell in a handcart with my feet up and smoking a cigar. Bring it on baby, bring it on.

94

Islamic Cultural Terrorism

June 15, 2011

Anyone criticising the religion of peace is likely to be accused of stirring up hatred, although I prefer to think of it as stirring up common sense, which appears to have sunk without trace in recent years to the bottom of a swamp of political correctness.

Besides, if you really want to stir up hatred you just have to open a copy of the Koran and start preaching.

In a previous video I tried to point out that the Koran, like the Bible, contains many peaceful verses and that if people focused on them a bit more things might be different, but I reckoned without the principle of abrogation, which means that the later violent verses supersede the earlier peaceful ones. So you can talk about a religion of peace all you like, but you're not supported by scripture. You say peace, the scripture says war, and the religion says conquest and domination.

And yes, we all know that not all Muslims push this agenda, but it's not the tiny minority that we keep hearing about. A third of Muslim students in Britain, for example, support killing in the name of their religion, and forty percent want to live under sha-ria. That's a minority, yes, but there's nothing tiny about it. And this is why Islam would be a problem in the West even without the help of its leftist enablers, because it is a supremacist ideol-ogy that feels entitled to expand using aggressive intimidation, or what I call cultural terrorism. Anyone who criticises Islam publicly can expect to be threatened with physical violence. If that's not terrorism, then what is it?

In the world of the cultural terrorist, if you oppose the oppression of women and minorities, you're an enemy of religious freedom; if you despise violent superstition, you're a racist; and if you reject religious totalitarianism you have a mental illness.

Let me tell you something: when you get to the stage where anyone criticising your beliefs is automatically deemed to have a mental illness, that is a sure sign of mental illness. It's also cultural terrorism.

The word "Islamophobia" is cultural terrorism in action. It's provably statistically false as a concept. The number of Muslims who are attacked or abused for who they are is small compared with other groups and it simply doesn't warrant a special word.

In some parts of northern Europe, Muslims are actually the majority perpetrators of violent attacks, and in the city of Oslo in Norway all the rapes in that city in the last three years, all of them, were committed by Muslim immigrants using rape as a weapon of cultural terrorism.

The word "Islamophobia" is pure political opportunism, and pure cultural terrorism, intended, like all terrorism, to intimidate people, in this case into shame and silence. And I think that anyone in the West who uses that word for any reason other than to ridicule it should seriously examine their conscience, especially if they're female or gay.

"Racist" used to be a powerful word that would have stopped any civilised person in their tracks, but now when I hear it my initial reflex is to think less of the person using it, and to wish they would invest in a dictionary to save embarrassing themselves any further.

Nobody is a racist for objecting to religious privilege, or for wanting everyone to obey the same laws, or for wanting full and equal human rights for everyone without exception. And nobody is a racist for not wanting to eat the cruelty of halal-slaughtered meat without being told about it, or for asking someone to show their face in public, or for not wanting to be treated by hospital staff who haven't washed their hands properly because of their stupid religion. And nobody is a racist for asking the police to do their job and uphold the law.

Two thousand young girls in Britain were genitally mutilated last year, a crime that's supposed to carry a fourteen-year prison sentence. Nobody has been prosecuted, because police and social workers don't want to cause offence and damage community relations. How thoughtful. How sensitive. Damaging a few thousand young girls, on the other hand, or should I say maiming them for life, is apparently a price worth paying for "community cohesion" – or should that be cultural terrorism?

In the London borough of Tower Hamlets, which has now been completely taken over by Islamic extremists, and where the police are afraid to do their job because doing their job might be Islamophobic, cultural terrorism is practised openly, with gay people attacked and abused in the streets, women threatened with murder for not covering their face, and just recently a teacher was beaten into a coma with a brick, a knife and a metal rod for having the temerity to be a non-Muslim teaching religion to children. This is what Islamic cultural terrorism brings, and is bringing to cities all over Europe.

If the far right were behaving like this you just know the police would be all over them. Well, I've got news for the Tower Hamlets police: this is the far right, the religious far right, and it doesn't get any further right (or further wrong) than that.

The relentless erosion of free speech we've witnessed in recent years has been achieved through Islamic cultural terrorism. In other words, by the threat of a violent response.

Free speech used to mean you can say what you like as long as it's true. Now, thanks to cultural terrorism, it means you can say what you like as long as it doesn't offend Muslims, as people all over Europe are finding out to their cost.

Islam doesn't like free speech because Islam is afraid of the truth, and with good reason, because the truth is that a growing number people in the West find this religion and everything it represents deeply offensive. We find its message deeply offen sive, its values deeply offensive, its treatment of women deeply offensive, and its attitude to homosexuals, Jews and anyone who isn't a Muslim deeply offensive, yet nobody is offering us any compensation for hurt feelings.

Everything about this wretched religion violates everything we believe in. We'd have to be stupid not to dislike it, and we'd have to be crazy to respect it. And no, we don't need to be educated about Islam. We already know more about it than we want to know, and we know enough to wish we had never heard of it. And that is one hundred percent the fault of Islam, the religion of aggressive intolerance, the religion of phoney grievances, tantrums, violent threats and more tantrums – the religion of cultural terrorism.

95

Name the Poison

June 22, 2011

OK, I've been contacted this week by several people in Norway pointing out that the rape figures I used in my last video were misleading, as it was only assault rapes that were carried out exclusively by non-western immigrants, a category that doesn't include domestic rape or date rape, something the news report didn't make clear, but which I'm happy to make clear now.

And what this means is that those women who were attacked and raped in the street by strangers were victims of non-western immigrants, with the rapist in the video specifically citing his religion as justification, and claiming that his religion entitles him to treat women any way he likes.

Can anyone guess what religion that might be?

I'll give you a clue: in countries where this religion calls the shots a woman who is raped is likely to be charged with adultery and thrown in prison. She'll need four male witnesses to prove the charge when the only male witnesses likely to be available are the rapists themselves. The testimony of women and non-Muslims is not allowed.

In this way, by making it almost impossible for a raped woman to receive justice, the religion of Islam condones and encourages rape.

Right now an Australian woman is suing her own government for giving her inadequate consular advice about what might happen if she reported being raped in the United Arab Emirates. What did happen is that she was charged with adultery and thrown in prison for eight months. She's lucky it didn't happen in Saudi Arabia or she'd have had a hundred lashes on top of it, or in Iran, where she might have been stoned to death.

There are many reasons why the religion of Islam impoverishes western society, but the main one, in my opinion, is that it degrades and debases women – except, of course, for left-wing women who happily degrade and debase themselves defending Islam like turkeys defending Christmas.

A woman in Islam needs to be covered from head to toe because men are not expected to exhibit any kind of basic self-control. I get a lot of correspondence from angry Muslim males, and I've lost count of the number of times I've been told that western women are asking to be raped because of the way they dress.

No other religion teaches people to think like this.

Recently here in Britain, we've had a rash of Muslim gangs pimping and raping young girls in northern England. I do mean Muslim gangs, not Asians, as the media keep reporting. There are no Sikhs or Hindus involved in this, and to call them Asians to avoid naming the real problem is a slander on Hindus and Sikhs.

These men do it because they regard non-Muslim women as subhuman trash. And this poison is coming directly from their religion, a religion whose values are dictated and imposed by some of the most narrow-minded, psychotic human beings on this planet. (And coming, as I do, from an Irish Catholic background, believe me, that's saying something.)

And it's not just white western girls they target. Hindu and Sikh girls get the same treatment because they're not Muslims, so they too are regarded as trash.

But nobody wants to name the problem. We keep dancing around it with euphemism and evasion for fear of causing offence.

Well, then, I'll name it, shall I? It's Islam. That's the problem. Good, I'm glad we've got that cleared up.

All over the Islamic world, men are raised from the cradle to believe they have a perfect right to treat women any way they like. In Pakistan, where the northern England rapists come from, a thousand women a year are murdered in so-called honour killings, and a woman who tries to report a rape is likely to be raped again in the police station, they take the matter so lightly.

The fact that we import this mentality at all would be bad enough, but what compounds it, what makes it immeasurably worse, is our blind refusal to name the poison at the heart of it, the poison that drives it forward, which is Islam's fundamental view of women as inferior human beings.

This is not just unacceptable, it's not just wrong, it's obscene. It's as obscene as any openly racist political platform, and should be regarded with the same contempt.

So why isn't it? Because it's easier for us to filter Islamic misogyny through a convenient multicultural lens that absolves us of all responsibility. It's easier to respect difference and celebrate diversity than it is to grow a backbone. And it's easier to pretend we stand for something and to wear our phoney relativist virtue like a pathetic badge of honour than it is to tell the truth and name the poison.

It needs to be named. It needs to be shamed. It needs to be confronted and challenged, openly, loudly and often, without apology, until it's eliminated forever, for the sake of all humanity. And if we in the West won't do it, then who will?

And yes, some Muslims will be offended, because some Muslims are always offended, but they'll be OK when they get used to it.

96

An Illiberal Consensus

July 4, 2011

The Islamic fanatics who are such a nuisance in the West wouldn't be half the problem they are without the complicity of the multiculti metropolitan middle-class left who are all too eager to curtail free speech and suppress inconvenient ideas by misrepresenting them as bigotry and racism.

Here in Britain we've known for some time that the BBC's reputation for impartial news reporting has been pretty much destroyed by this kind of political correctness.

The truth is no longer sacred to the BBC. It's now seen as a problem to be navigated around with euphemism, as in the case of Islamic terrorism, or simply dismissed with crude slanders like "far-right" when it comes to political views the BBC disapproves of. Recently, for example, Geert Wilders was acquitted by a court in Amsterdam, but not, it seems, by the BBC who, I notice, still insist on referring to him as a far-right politician, which is such an outrageous slur it ought to be actionable.

Nazis and racists are far-right. Anyone would think they

were talking about Hitler. You really have to wonder how some of these people have the nerve to call themselves journalists.

Millions of people trust the BBC as a source of impartiality and truth. Yet, according to the BBC website, the Dutch people have elected somebody on a par with a Nazi to help govern them. The words 'far-right' appear in the very first sentence of the report, telling the reader straight away: "This is somebody we disapprove of, and we suggest that you disapprove of them as well. And you know you can trust us. We're the BBC."

Except that we can't trust the BBC. Those days have gone. We can't trust the BBC to look at a thing impartially and tell the simple truth, because the truth is that the BBC is no longer an impartial organisation. It now has a cultural and political agenda because it's full to the rafters with multiculti metropolitan middle-class left-wing pricks, or what we in Britain call Guardianistas – people who see their mirror image in the *Guardian* newspaper, which lives and breathes multiculturalism, diversity and all things middle-class left-wing prick, and where the BBC advertises for its multiculti middle-class left-wing staff.

The *Guardian* is such a biased multiculti middle-class left-wing rag it could be Swedish, and, in newspaper terms, it doesn't get any more damning than that.

As well as being an open platform for Hamas propaganda, the *Guardian* is the natural home of the terminally tolerant. It's characterised by a smug and patronising political correctness that, by default, blames western society, and especially America, for everything that's wrong with this world. It's the paper of choice for relativist wackos like feminists who defend female genital mutilation on cultural grounds or who endorse the Islamic veil as a symbol of female empowerment. It's for people who know some perfectly normal decent Muslims and therefore Islam can't possibly be a threat to anybody, and anyone who disagrees is being unhelpful and should be silenced. It's for people who are passionate about diversity, even though they all went to the same universities, read the same books, and have the same dopey opinions about everything. And it's for people who just love the Palestinians because it gives them the chance to be anti-Semitic at dinner parties without offending left-wing Jews.

The *Guardian* and the BBC are both pillars of a kind of British metropolitan multiculti middle-class left-wing prickocracy whose days are numbered.

People are getting tired of being made to feel like criminals for holding the wrong opinion, and there's a massive backlash coming against political correctness, especially when all those young people who are having it rammed down their throats by middle-class left-wing pricks in universities all over the western world finally grow up and start thinking for themselves. It will be like getting rid of lead poisoning.

Meanwhile, the *Guardian's* politics are its own business. It's a private company and nobody is forced to buy the wretched thing. But the BBC is a publicly funded national broadcaster – funded, moreover, by an indiscriminate poll tax that hits the poorest hardest. It has a duty to reflect the views and values of everyone it purports to serve, and not just the views and values of the multiculti middle-class left-wing pricks who happen to work there.

It also has a duty to the public to tell the simple truth unvarnished with bias and spin. We can get that anywhere else, thank you very much. We pay for the BBC, and we deserve better.

We also deserve a better democracy as it happens, and, on a lighter note, I might as well tell you about another example we had recently of the patronising and condescending nature of the whole middle-class left-wing prick mentality.

A couple of months ago we had a referendum here in Britain to decide whether we should change the voting system.

The proposed new system, although by no means perfect, would have been more proportional. It drew support from a fairly wide political spectrum, and some very effective speakers from all shades of opinion could have been used to front the campaign and help it connect with people.

Unfortunately the campaign was organised by a bunch of middle-class left-wing pricks who arrogantly declined to draw on that support because they disapproved of some of the viewpoints, and, as a result, they blew the whole gig for everyone.

The people they did choose to front the campaign were all middle-class left-wing pricks like themselves; actors and other personalities in the media and the arts – people who inhabit a self-regarding bubble of advanced middle-class left-wing prickery and have no idea how despised their opinions really are.

Well, they found out. We all found out.

A few places known for their heavy concentration of middle-class left-wing pricks voted for the change. Everybody else, outside the bubble, voted against.

So now we're stuck with the old system permanently because the chances of getting another referendum are about as likely as finding fur on a fish, or getting unbiased news from the middle-class left-wing pricks at the *Guardian* or the **BBC**.

97

Insulting Religion

July 15, 2011

OK, this is a quick video for those, mainly Christians and Muslims, who keep telling me (for reasons I can never quite fathom) that I have no right to insult their religion.

I don't know who made up that rule when nobody was looking, but apparently somebody did, so let me give you my perspective on it now, if I may.

I give your religion as much respect as your religion gives me. There's nothing complicated about it. And I have every right to insult a religion that goes out of its way to insult, to judge and to condemn me as an inadequate human being, which your religion does with self-righteous gusto.

When it comes to insults, your religion started this, not me. If your religion kept its big mouth shut, then so would I. But given that it doesn't, and given the enormous amount of harm your religion has done in this world, I'd say that I have not only a right but a duty to insult it, as does every rational thinking person on this planet.

In fact, I think it should be compulsory for everyone to insult your religion every day. No, not every day – five times every day. Oh, what the hell – ten times. One for each commandment.

And even that wouldn't be enough, because the moment your religion claims any kind of jurisdiction over my experience you insult me at a level you can't even begin to comprehend. Even if your beliefs had substance, the arrogance of that would be insult enough, but the fact that they have no substance, but are merely a transparent raft of delusions and lies, magnifies the insult enormously.

And for this reason, not only do I have a perfect right to insult your religion, I have a right to insult you personally the moment I have to hear about your poxy religion.

The moment you offer me any kind of scripture-based opinion about what I should believe, or the values I should hold, or especially the morals I should exhibit, then you can expect to be graphically and comprehensively insulted for your trouble. And I sincerely hope it hurts your feelings, harms your emotional wellbeing, and damages your self-image to the extent that you have to go and lie down for ten minutes before you can even pray.

If I'm not allowed to express my sincerely held belief that your religion is a crock of dangerous evil dehumanising superstitious garbage, then it seems to me that I don't have religious freedom, but you do – because I can assure you that I hold that view with a passion and a solemn intensity that can match anything you've got to offer.

It is, for me, a core defining belief and a pillar of my whole reality, an absolutely unshakeable fundamental conviction that resonates to every fibre of my being, that your religion is, in fact, a crock of dangerous evil dehumanising superstitious garbage that pollutes and degrades the world I have to live in. And I'm not happy about it. And I feel morally obliged, nay, compelled, to make this known, loudly and often (regardless of who claims to be offended) because not to do so would violate everything I am and everything I believe in. I wouldn't be able to live with myself. I'd feel like a liar and a coward, and, well... something of a moral cockroach. And that would weigh very heavily on my conscience. I'm sure you understand.

98

Violence Is Not the Answer

July 27, 2011

The Norwegian murderer has shown himself to be as much an enemy of humanity as any jihadist. Indeed, he is a jihadist by any other name.

He claims there's a war going on, and there certainly is – a war between civilised people and violent barbarians like him.

It sickens me to think that this kind of thing can still happen when it must be obvious to even the most stupid among us that violence will never prevail, because it will never win the hearts and minds of the people, the ones who are always left to pick up the pieces. How obvious does it have to be? You'd have to be a moron not to see it – or a fanatic.

And, given the parlous state of democracy in Europe today, it's clear that any fundamental change in society is going to require overwhelming public support. Violence immediately snuffs that out like a candle. It's gone.

This lunatic has murdered seventy-six innocent people, and drawn hatred upon himself and everything he claims to believe in. He's hated in Norway. He's hated everywhere, as much as the suicide bombers in London and New York were hated, and still are, and as much as any fanatical zealot who thinks they have a right to play God.

Violence is not the answer. It's never the answer. And we will never progress as a species until we drag ourselves out of this swamp of violence. And that's why anyone who uses or who advocates violence for any political reason is my enemy. No exceptions.

I couldn't help noticing, however, in the aftermath of this atrocity, a rather unhealthy eagerness in some quarters to apportion blame by association, as if all critics of Islam are somehow complicit in this man's insanity. Well, that's very unfortunate, but, given that the rules have now clearly been changed in this regard, I'll be very interested to see how many hate-preaching imams are blamed for the next Islamic atrocity.

No one who criticises Islam or multiculturalism is in any way responsible for this lunatic's actions, and the criticisms are all still entirely valid. Islam is still a totalitarian ideology that actively threatens our freedom; political correctness is still, yes, cultural Marxism; and multiculturalism is still a lie. And, all over Europe, de facto blasphemy laws are still being used to prosecute people who criticise Islam, and only Islam.

These horrific murders have not changed any of that. And the only thing that will change it, and the only way to get the overwhelming public support needed for change, is not through violence, but by defending freedom of speech, no matter what, and by telling the truth. That's all we need.

99

Sharia Poster Boy

July 29, 2011

Well, we needed something to lift the gloom of the last week or so, and the comical side of religious fascism is nowhere more evident than in that ludicrous oaf, Andy Choudary, who has been up to his old tricks again with another publicity stunt and another bluff waiting to be called.

You'll remember Andy, of course. He's Britain's best known benefit-scrounging hate-preaching Islamist parasite. If you live in Britain, you pay all his bills for him. You pay his rent, you buy his groceries, you pay for his heating. Everything he needs is served up to him on a plate, courtesy of you, so that he can devote all his time to being a public nuisance.

And true to form, it seems that this week Andy and his little raggle-taggle army of aspiring mental patients have been going around putting up posters in the East End of London declaring the area a sharia-controlled zone. And this means no alcohol, no gambling, no music. None of the things that ordinary people like to do for entertainment in their free time will be allowed.

I must admit I was a bit disappointed to hear that the local authority immediately started taking down these posters. Typical bureaucrats, always want to spoil people's fun. They ought to be selling tickets for this one, because Andy and his little gang of bearded apes have made it clear that they intend to patrol the streets of east London enforcing sharia and preventing people from going about their lawful business.

I'll be interested to see how that works out for them, because I've known a few Eastenders in my time, and I can't think of anyone, with the possible exception of Geordies (that's people from Newcastle), who are less likely to tolerate having their pint of beer, their betting shop, and their song and dance interfered with by a bunch of puffed-up bearded blowfish in pyjamas.

And that's just the women.

So I say leave the posters up, let Andy and the boys patrol the streets, and let the games commence.

100

Britain Is a Riot

August 11, 2011

Who would be a police officer in Britain today? You'd need to have your head examined. You probably know that this week Britain has been terrorised by an underclass of welfare-dependent drug-addled criminal scum who have been allowed to run riot because the police haven't been allowed to do their job and protect the public.

The media is full of speculation about why it happened and what is the root cause. Well, that's easy. The root cause is stupidity, a complete lack of imagination, a stunted feral view of the world that amounts to self-inflicted moral and mental disablement, and it's the direct product of an entitlement culture that rewards idleness, encourages victimhood and compensates criminals. That's the root cause. It happened because there was nobody there to stop it, and because the people who did it know damn well that if they're caught they won't be properly punished. That's why it happened.

It also happened because we don't have enough police officers in Britain; they cost money, unfortunately. And many of the ones we do have are not properly trained in riot control, because that costs money.

It happened because police are not allowed to deal with rioting effectively in Britain using water cannon, tear gas, rubber bullets – the kind of things other riot police take for granted. Also, individual officers have learned from experience that if they lay a hand on a rioter they're likely to be charged with assault, or worse.

Ordinary officers in the police have got no chance at all. Whatever they do, they're criticised and vilified for it by people who are not in their situation, and who couldn't cope if they were.

When the rioting first broke out, if they had gone in straight away and started cracking heads, the media would have been all over them for police brutality.

They're not even allowed to carry guns, except in special circumstances, even though gun crime is rampant in Britain, and in some places it seems like every second fourteen-year-old is walking around with a gun jammed into a belt worn halfway down to his knees. Indeed, the whole thing happened because the police shot dead a man who was pointing a gun straight at them, and this apparently inflamed local sensitivities, which is the worst crime you can commit as a policeman in modern Britain.

The social justice brigade have been quick to blame the rioting on the usual suspects: inequality, unfairness and lack of opportunity.

"This is happening," they say, "because these youngsters are unemployed." No, it isn't. Who needs a job when you can deal drugs? That's where the real money is. Besides, if they had to look for employment they might have to learn to read and write.

"OK, then, it's happening because they're disengaged from society."

Oh, are they? How awful for them. Hey, come to think of it, that might have something to do with all the drugs.

A TV reporter actually stopped one of them in the street and asked him why he was doing it, and he replied: "I've got no money."

And I thought: "Aw, isn't that awful? My heart goes out to the poor little lad. He's got no money because he spent all his money on a BlackBerry phone and a gram of heroin, innit."

You've got money, you parasites. You get state benefits because other people work to pay for your room and board. You've got no job because you're unemployable, and that's because you're inadequate. You've got no backbone, no morals, no knowledge, no intelligence, and you can't be trusted. You're like rats who shit in their own nest. And you'll never make anything of yourselves because there's nothing there to begin with. And for that you can blame your stupid ignorant parents, not your lack of opportunity.

There are people on this planet who can only dream of your lack of opportunity, you disgusting parasitical halfwits. Go tell the starving people in Somalia that you've got no opportunity. Tell the ten-year-old in Pakistan making mud bricks eighteen hours a day for no pay – tell these people that you have no opportunity, you pathetic pampered human vermin.

If we had any kind of justice system worth the name in this country, anyone convicted of taking part in these riots would automatically lose entitlement to state benefit for life and their house would be demolished. That would be justice. And if it violated their human rights, hey, so much the better.

However, what will happen, if past form is anything to go by, is that a few hundred dregs of society will go through the courts and get derisory sentences, while the rest of them take their new plasma TVs and go back to their normal lives terrorising the people around them, which they can do because there's nobody there to stop them.

And then everything will go back to normal for everyone except the victims, the people who have been murdered or who have been burnt out of home and business, because the police weren't there to protect them, because there aren't enough of them and because they're not allowed to.

101

Europe Needs a Revolution

August 25, 2011

We are the first generation of Europeans who have never had to defend their freedom, and, as a consequence, we now take freedom so much for granted it has become a root assumption about reality, so that even when we can see it being taken away from us, we simply don't believe it.

The Euro bailout fiasco is proving that you can't make a currency omelette without wrecking a few economies, but still by far the most worthless currency in Europe today is the vote. A wheelbarrow full of votes won't buy you a say in the lawmaking process, and that's why this crisis is happening.

It's also why Europe needs a revolution. Nothing as crude as an armed uprising – I'm not suggesting anything like that. I mean a revolution of public will and intent to restore the power of the ballot box to the people from whom it has been stolen, because, at the risk of sounding like an extremist, there's nothing wrong with Europe today that couldn't be cured by more democracy.

It's ironic that, just as the Arabs are finally claiming their right to self-determination, we in Europe are busy handing ours away. Or rather, we're having it signed away by a political class who openly despise the people they purport to represent. Soon the Arabs will be lecturing us on democracy.

The artificial single currency is regarded as an essential prelude to full undemocratic political union in Europe, and Germany has done more than any country to prop it up, because, as the Chancellor said, it's Germany's "historic duty to protect the euro".

This is Eurospeak for residual war guilt.

The Germans don't have a historic duty to do anything except mind their own business (and maybe make a point of staying out of Poland).

If I was German I would resent my government's desire to keep making amends for something that had nothing to do with anyone alive today, and to pay for it with my money. The best thing Germany could do for other countries is to let them stand on their own feet. As it is, the German government is creating a mini economic empire of vassal states, and setting its country up to be hated and resented all over again. Nice work, Mrs Merkel.

The European Union is not, in fact, a union at all, but a continent-wide political coup. What began as a common market has now metamorphosed by stealth into a supranational political dictatorship, a parasitical organism living on the backs of the European nation states, sucking their life blood, and slowly killing them off; a bureaucratic tyranny that wants to "harmonise" out of existence the national identities that have made Europe a continent of genuine diversity and a cultural crucible whose values have shaped the entire western world.

But they want to put an stop to all that in the European Union of Soviet Socialist Republics, which is why European laws are never enacted in response to any kind of organic need in society, but as top-down directives intended to impose indiscriminate uniformity for its own sake. More than fifty percent of British law is now made this way by people we haven't elected and can't remove. And, as they can override our elected politicians whenever they like, it's only a matter of time before it's a hundred percent.

We pay the European Union more than fifteen billion pounds a year, and rising. That's more than twice all the public service cuts combined. We squander that every year, and all we get for it is ordered around.

Thanks to unqualified and politically motivated European judges, we can no longer deport foreign terrorists and criminals from Britain, no matter what crimes they've committed, in case it violates their human rights. Yet, under the European Arrest Warrant, a British citizen can be extradited on no evidence to face charges that are not even crimes in Britain, and to be held without charge for months in appalling conditions without anyone having made a case against them. No human rights for them. And British judges can do nothing about this, even if they want to, which they seldom do, to be fair. And not one of the three main political parties in Britain is prepared to give the people a chance to have a say about any of this, because they know damn well what we would say.

I'm beginning to understand how Americans must have felt

living under King George. What was that again, no taxation without representation?

The War of Independence wasn't America against England. It was Englishmen resisting the oppressive regime of their autocratic German king – asserting their human rights, in modern parlance.

America may be a melting pot now, but it began with the defence of age-old English liberties – liberties that were promptly written into the Constitution, something we never got around to doing in Britain, so we no longer enjoy the same liberties Americans do. We don't have a constitution. We don't have a First Amendment. What we have, and what the whole of Europe has, is the Lisbon Treaty, a kind of top-down constitution that has been imposed on us against our will. And, unlike the American Constitution which empowers the people, the European constitution disempowers the people and empowers the unelected bureaucrats and career politicians for whose sole benefit it was created.

Whatever the reality of the Republican–Democrat stitch-up, America is still governed, at least in theory, by the people and for the people. No such pretence exists any more in Europe, where the people have had to stand by watching helplessly, their protests ignored, as their elected representatives sign away their sovereignty and their franchise without permission and burden them with a mountain of phoney debt they did not incur.

If a lawyer or an accountant behaved like that they would end up in prison, but the political class get away with it because they make up the rules as they go along. They are literally a law unto themselves. The ink was barely dry on the wretched Lisbon

Treaty when they were violating its terms to throw even more of other people's money at economies they've destroyed.

Most of these people have never had a proper job outside politics. And it shows. They inhabit a bubble of their own creation, like a priesthood, and, in taking away the power of the ballot box as they have, they've removed the people's ability to prick that bubble and let in a little reality.

In short, they've stolen our birthright, and that of our children and grandchildren, and that's why Europe needs a revolution.

And if ultimately these criminals are not held to account by the law, as they ought to be, they will certainly be held to account by history as the generation that tried to snuff out democracy in Europe. A generation of traitors, of incompetent self-serving political pipsqueaks who call themselves leaders, yet who have shown they wouldn't know how to lead a pack of lemmings straight over a cliff.

Actually, I take that back. That's exactly what they are doing.

102

In Superstition We Trust

September 7, 2011

It's well known that America has taken the Christian religion to a level of bovine credulity that really hasn't been seen since the Middle Ages, so I was a little surprised to hear this week that the country is becoming less religious.

Back in the 1950s, ninety-nine percent of Americans said they believed in God. Now it's only ninety-three percent. What a shocking spiritual and moral decline. It must feel as if the place is falling apart.

In reality, of course, compared with other western countries, America is still rabidly religious. Aggressively and insanely religious, some would say. It has, in fact, elevated religion to a dark comic art form. It is, after all, the home of the Bible Belt, a kind of atheist heart of darkness. It's the home of sideshow Christianity with its fake healings and creation museums and slippery conmen speaking in tongues – all of them forked. It's the home of corporate Christianity and the televangelism industry. Send money now in Jesus' name. (What was that third commandment again?) God is on the money, and he's very much in the money, and he had better be on every politician's lips if they know what's good for them.

It's hard for us to imagine an American politician making any kind of fundamental statement about their country without invoking God. And we're likely to be hearing a fair amount of that in the next few months, because the presidential campaign is under way and it looks as if Jesus is getting the Republican nomination again.

Wouldn't it be nice if, just for once, the Republican Party could find a credible candidate who isn't walking around with Jesus on their shoulder like a goddamned parrot?

The current front runner is Texas governor Rick Perry, whose budget is balanced, but we're not so sure about his mind.

He believes in teaching creationism in schools, and he opened his campaign with a prayer rally organised with the help of some fundamentalist wackos who want to see a Christian army take dominion over the American government, and ultimately the whole of society. In Jesus' name, of course. Kind of a Christian Taliban deal. Oh, and they're also very big on demons.

So, given all this, if I was an American voter I wouldn't care if Rick Perry could balance a budget on a high wire over Niagara Falls, I wouldn't want him in the White House.

Mind you, I wouldn't want the current guy in there either, because he's a European by instinct, and he wants to take America in that direction.

Big government, high taxes and a massive welfare state is the European way. They call it social democracy, and you can see what it's done for us. If you look at the size of Britain's welfare bill you'd think half the country was disabled. It's a rotten system and a drain on society, and that's why, if I was an American I'd vote for Satan before I'd vote for Obama, but Jesus? That might be a step too far.

Obama or Jesus? It's the choice from hell.

I remember when Obama was first elected he had a halo just like Jesus. Whatever happened to that?

Anyway, despite the shocking decline of religion in America, at this stage the only thing we know for sure about the next president is that they will not be an atheist. Forty-nine percent of Americans say they would not vote for an atheist candidate, which makes an atheist president about as likely as a Protestant pope. It also makes the United States a country where politicians are afraid not to believe in God, or to pretend they do. Although the Constitution makes a point of keeping religion and politics separate, in practice it's impossible to be a successful politician without sucking up to religion. (You know, that thing that's in such decline.)

As if to underline this, in another poll we hear that thirty percent of Americans believe the Bible is the literal word of God. That's like hearing that thirty percent of fifteen-year-olds believe in Santa Claus. Well, it is to me, anyway.

A further forty-three percent believe the Bible is the inspired word of God, and only seventeen percent believe it's just a book of fables and legends.

So eighty-three percent of adult Americans believe the Bible is either directly or indirectly the word of God, which makes you wonder how many of them have actually read it.

If the Bible is the word of God it's bad news for humanity, because it shows a god who is contradictory, ill-focused and incoherent; a god who finds it impossible to simply state what he means in plain language. In short, somebody who can't be trusted.

Fortunately, it's not the word of God, for two very good reasons. One: because God doesn't exist. And I can say that with authority (well, with as much authority as anyone who says he does exist). And two: because the Bible is self-evidently a collection of different books written at different times in different styles by different people. It is entirely of human origin. It was written by men and put together by men. Some books got in, and others didn't. All the editorial decisions were made by men, for the purpose of controlling other men. That purpose has now been served. Everyone involved is long dead and buried, and their ideas have no more jurisdiction over us than our half-baked ideas will over those who will live a thousand years from now. Imagine us trying to dictate to those people from our pit of ignorance how they should engage with reality. And now imagine the withering contempt they would rightly show for that suggestion.

Given its history and format, I'd say the Bible has less chance of being the word of God than just about any book you can think of. But then again, surely eighty-three percent of Americans can't be wrong. Oh, I don't know. More than eighty-three percent of Americans regularly vote Republican or Democrat, and they've yet to pick a winner between them. So I don't know what to think any more.

Might as well look on the bright side, and the good news is that only forty-nine percent of Americans wouldn't vote for an atheist, which means a clear majority would. What a break-through. At this rate it might only be a couple of hundred years before you don't need to pander to superstition and juju to become electable in the world's most powerful country. This could be the beginning of a whole new enlightenment. O happy day.

103

The Great Palestinian Lie

October 6, 2011

Is it racist to criticise the Palestinians as the world's most tiresome crybabies with a bogus cause and a plight that's entirely self-inflicted? I bet it is. I wouldn't be surprised if it was against the law in certain European countries. But I'm going to do it anyway, because somebody has to.

And I realise I'll probably lose a few friends with this video, but that's OK. Friends like that I can do without.

All any of us can do is to tell the truth as we see it. I mean as we actually see it, and not as we think we're supposed to see it. The worst thing we can do is to see the truth and tell a lie, and I see the Palestinian cause as a lie; a lie designed to exploit western liberal guilt, like the lie of Islamophobia, and the lie of the mythical religion of peace that nobody has ever seen in action.

I used to be a lot more critical of Israel and I used to believe there was a fairly simple two-state solution because I used to believe the Arabs were acting in good faith. I still want to believe that, but the evidence tells me I'd be a fool to believe it.

I've seen that every concession Israel makes is met with more demands and more excuses not to negotiate. They could have had peace ten times over if they wanted it, but they don't want peace; they want victory, and they won't be happy until Israel is wiped from the map. A member of Fatah's central committee said as much on television recently, but as he said, they keep that to themselves and tell the rest of the world a different story.

And, as part of that story, the bogus claim for Palestinian statehood is currently passing through the United Nations, and we're all waiting to see what plops out the other end. Not that it really matters, because, despite what the Palestinian public relations industry (i.e. the western media) might tell you, this is not about territory, and it certainly isn't about justice or human rights because Arab societies don't know the meaning of those words. It's about Jew-hatred, as mandated by the Koran, and as preached in the mosques and taught to the children in Arab countries day in and day out, generation after poisoned generation.

The Arabs don't hate Jews because of Israel. They hate Israel because of Jews.

The situation in the West Bank and Gaza exists because forty-five years ago several Arab countries attacked Israel unprovoked with overwhelming odds because it was a Jewish state. If it hadn't been a Jewish state, they wouldn't have attacked. And they attacked with the intention of wiping it from the map and committing genocide. But they failed, because the Jews had a bit more steel in their blood than the Arabs bargained for, and who could be surprised after what they had been through, and after seeing how the rest of the world had responded to their plight? Large numbers of Jews could have escaped the Nazis if they

219

had somewhere else to go, but other countries wouldn't let them in. The Mufti of Jerusalem at the time was a friend of Hitler's, and, good Muslim that he was, he approved of the final solution, and had plans for his own holocaust in the Middle East once the Nazis had won the war.

So who can blame the Israelis today for defending themselves as if they mean it, when they're dealing with people they know they can't trust, and who they know hate them enough to want to exterminate them as a people? Anybody else in their position would behave the same way. I know I would, and I wouldn't apologise for it.

Israel is surrounded by enemies. Peace is more in their interest than in anyone else's, which is why they keep making concessions. But it's not in the interest of the Palestinian leadership. Peace is the last thing they want. They need to keep the pot boiling. They need to keep their people angry and resentful and hating Jews. Peace would ruin everything, because they won't be happy until Israel has been wiped from the map and the Jews have been driven into the sea.

If they really believe that's going to happen they're insane. And if they don't really believe it, they're even more insane, wouldn't you say?

And all you good-hearted western liberals who keep banging the drum for the poor Palestinians, I sympathise with you because you're doing it for the right reason, but you're being used and exploited, just as the people in the West Bank and Gaza are being exploited, by people who have no intention of negotiating peace because they're driven primarily by crude irrational religious hatred.

When you protest for Palestine you know you'll be in the company of people calling for Jews to be gassed. Do you think that's an accident?

You're dealing with something here beyond politics and beyond reason, something truly ugly that drives a spike through all your cosy left/right assumptions, and your naivety is helping to stoke it like bellows to a fire.

The world needs to stop pretending that Palestine is about justice and human rights, and have the moral courage to call this thing what it is, to put a stop to this charade, this endless dance around a non-existent negotiating table.

We need to do the Arabs a huge favour and tell them the truth they so badly need to hear, that their hatred is the cause of their misery. They've become prisoners of it. It has come to define their very identity. And until they can find a way to remove this ugly stain from their hearts, they'll always be chained to it, and they, and their children, will never be free – Arab spring or no Arab spring.

Peace? How many wasted generations of hate do you think it will take?

104

Halloween Burka

October 28, 2011

We're coming up to Halloween again, the time of year when we like to put aside our troubles for a few hours to celebrate all things dark and evil.

If you like dressing up in ghoulish outfits on Halloween, and if you're looking to wear something a little different this year (and something truly evil), then forget about the zombie masks and vampire teeth. Go the whole hog and get yourself a burka.

The Islamic cloak of death has to be the ultimate Halloween garment, if only because it's so versatile. You could fit it with a pair of bat wings; that would look rather good. Or you could simply carry a scythe to represent death, of course. I think both ideas would work very well. Or, if you prefer something a bit more authentic, you could carry around a baby with rickets, or a sign saying: "Freedom go to hell" or "USA you will pay".

The burka is a remarkable garment, in that it covers the face while allowing all the ugliness through, so, despite the anonymity it gives, you might just as well be sporting a big old gap-toothed pumpkin-headed grin with a light of demonic insanity burning from within.

But you know me. I always like to find the good in everybody and everything, and one good thing about wearing a burka is that it will significantly reduce your chances of being raped on the night, and who can say that's a bad thing? It just goes to show there's good to be found in everything if you look for it, even in something as disgusting, degrading and dehumanising as the Islamic shroud of cowardly male misogyny and oppression.

And, by the way, I hope I didn't offend any western feminists with that remark. I know how touchy some of you girls can get when anyone criticises Islamic male supremacism.

Of course, if you want to be really super safe (because we all know what men are like) you'd be even less likely to get raped if you went around inside a wooden box. You could put it on rollers so your feet don't have to stick out in a provocative and licentious way. Although, on reflection, that might be taking things just a bit too far. Chances are you'll be perfectly OK with the mobile tent, but you might want to have a carpenter standing by just in case.

Obviously nobody wants to cause religious offence, so, if you decide to wear a burka on Halloween you might want to distinguish your Halloween burka from a regular Islamic burka by decorating it with primitive supernatural symbols, like, oh I dunno, crescent moons, perhaps, something like that. Or you may decide that a skull and crossbones motif is more appropriate. It really is a blank canvas.

I certainly hope the idea takes off, because I think western society would be culturally enriched (for a change) if everybody went around in a burka on Halloween. It would certainly help to lighten the rather creepy and sinister image of this alien garment if we took the annual opportunity that Halloween affords to openly mock and ridicule it as the clownish symbol of male inadequacy and stupidity it really is, and that would inevitably lead to greater mutual understanding, which is something I think we all want. And who knows, it might even persuade extremist Muslims to laugh at themselves. (Well, there's a first time for everything.) And why not? After all, everybody else is laughing at them. Surely it would be divisive and drive a wedge between communities if they were to exclude themselves from all the fun just because they've got no sense of humour.

105

Useful Idiots for Palestine

November 4, 2011

Well, incredibly I'm still getting a very heated response to my video about the phoney Palestinian cause and the rabid anti-Semitism that drives it. Quite a lot of shouty upper-case emails calling me a Zionist shill, a Shabbos goy (that's a good one, isn't it?), and of course all the usual favourites – Nazi, racist and so on.

It's getting so that if I don't get called a racist at least once a day I begin to worry that I may be doing something wrong, so please keep it up, folks. You're doing a great job. And this video is just for you, because, predictably, nowhere in this blizzard of spittle-flecked abuse has anybody bothered to address the central point of the video, which is that irrational Islamic Jew-hatred is the root cause of the problem in the Middle East, and you would have to be blind or politically constipated (in other words, an Islamised lefty) not to see that, or not to want to see it.

It's often said, because it's true, that if the Arabs laid down their weapons there would be peace; if the Jews laid down their weapons they would be massacred, because the Arabs (that's the Muslim Arabs for all you hair-splitters out there) don't want peace – they want the Jews dead.

They could have their own state by now if they wanted it, but they don't want it. They want an end to the Jewish state. And, thanks to their religion (the religion of peace), they have the same delusions of manifest destiny in this regard, and the same grisly agenda as Hitler. If they had the wherewithal they would commit genocide today. They wouldn't wait till tomorrow.

It's not even a secret. Thanks to the internet, we can all now see the kind of stuff that gets broadcast regularly on Arab TV praising the Holocaust and demonising Jews in disgusting ways that would be illegal in any civilised country.

We know how much the Arabs hate Jews. They can't stop talking about it. They drum it into their children for all the world to see, brainwashing them into becoming suicide bombers. We can see little three-year-olds being taught that Jews are apes and pigs and how glorious it is to be an Islamic martyr and kill yourself to kill Jews. And that's what you support when you support the Palestinians, and you'll have to live with your conscience, that's if you can find one, because we all know that when operating from the twisted moral perspective of the Islamised political left, having a conscience, or a backbone for that matter, isn't always possible.

Like all things Islamic, the Palestinians have long been officially above criticism in the West, and the terrorists of Hamas have plenty of friends, especially in places like Norway and Sweden, whose governments and media seem to hate Israel almost as much as they hate their own countries.

Although Jew-hatred has always been part of European culture, thanks largely to the Catholic Church, Norway and Sweden are now getting serious reputations as almost Islamically anti-Semitic. Obviously that doesn't apply to everybody in those countries, but it does apply to the governments and the media who control and slant the information people get, and who do their best to demonise Israel out of all proportion to reality in the minds of the people.

And the people? Well, it's a curious thing about the western world in general – nobody trusts the media, yet everybody believes what the media tell them.

So, although I sometimes get the feeling that half the people in the West would almost applaud if Iran were to attack Israel with a nuclear bomb, in Norway and Sweden, God bless them, they'd probably hold street parties.

So it was no surprise to me that these two were among the western countries who shamefully refused to boycott the recent UN anti-racism hatefest, Durban III, where some of the world's most vile racists, child murderers, child rapists, slavers, war criminals, terrorist funders and serial human rights violators got together to slander and vilify a genuine democracy where Arabs have more rights than they do in any Arab country, including the ones supposedly liberated in the so-called Arab spring – like Libya, where they've announced that their new constitution will be based on sharia (sorry girls, no liberation for you) and where, true to form, they've already started torturing and murdering people. Oh, and they've also made it known that Jews (not Israelis, Jews) will not be welcome in the new Libya. Surprise surprise.

Next door in Egypt where, since the revolution, hundreds of Christians have been murdered in the streets by the army for the crime of not being Muslims, if those wretched people have anything to be grateful for, it's for the fact that they're not Jewish, because, if they were, none of them would be left alive. And that's what you support when you support the Palestinians, because it's not about Israel, it's about Jews.

In universities all over the western world, Muslim Brotherhood front groups are allowed to spread their anti-Semitic poison unchecked, while anyone defending Israel is shouted down or barred from access altogether, because students who have been Islamised don't like free speech.

Whenever Israel defends itself from terrorism we see armies of self-righteous left-wing bubble heads marching through European cities holding banners that read: "We are all Hamas now", as if that's something to be proud of.

If those banners were honest they would read: "We are all religious hate-mongers, racists and murderers now, who put no value on human life because our minds are pickled in a barbaric religion and we are completely insane."

Actually, that's a bit of a mouthful, isn't it, so maybe the last bit could go on a separate banner or something. Or why not simply cut to the chase and put: "Death to Jews", because that's what you support when you support the Palestinians. You're being used as a hand puppet by the Muslim Brotherhood because you've chosen to believe the lie of the apartheid state without bothering to examine the evidence. You've bought a propaganda campaign Goebbels would have been proud of, and what you're actually doing is supporting an Islamic war of extermination against Jews. And, if you measure yourself by the same stringent standards that you left-wing hypocrites love to apply to others, then it follows that you are a racist with blood on your hands. No offence.

106

The Gathering Storm

November 29, 2011

Europe is in the northern hemisphere, so I guess the European Union will go anti-clockwise when it finally goes down the plug-hole, because that is where it's going.

Like the Soviet Union before it, this monster is now visibly collapsing under the weight of its own illegitimacy, and the only question is: Will it end peacefully by democratic means, or will it end in tears and blood?

You don't need to be a student of history, or of human nature, to see something very ugly coming down the road in Europe if things go on as they are. There has already been social unrest in Greece, and there will be social unrest in other countries as people wake up and realise what's being done to them, and what has been stolen from them.

When you deny people a voice and disconnect them from the governing process, you close a safety valve, and, unless it's opened again, you've guaranteed that sooner or later there will be an explosion.

People sometimes say to me: "You're supposed to be an atheist, yet you're always talking about politics." Yes, that's because I'm an atheist who believes in democracy. I'm sorry if that's a difficult idea to understand, but I'm sure if you persevere with it you'll be just fine.

I live in a country within the European Union, though, so I find I believe in democracy in much the way a person might believe in God – more in hope than in certainty. Luckily, I have faith.

I don't regard it as an end in itself, however, because I realise that democracy is far from perfect, but, from what I've seen, it's the only form of government that can be trusted with our freedom, and that I do regard as an end in itself.

The absence of democracy is the reason everything has gone pear-shaped here in Europe. Time after time, the people have made it clear that they wanted to go one way and their self-appointed unelected masters have pushed them in the opposite direction with a fanatical zeal that can only be called religious.

Impervious to reason or to evidence, they've insisted on pushing blindly ahead, no matter what, as much in denial as any creationist.

They're like medieval doctors who, when the patient fails to respond to an application of leeches, insist that the only remedy is to apply yet more leeches. As a consequence, we have in Europe today the worst of all possible worlds, a kind of mutant statist corporate socialism imposed from above by an unaccountable dogma-obsessed political priesthood.

The more power they get, the more they want, and the more they take. So far, we've seen two democratically elected prime ministers removed from office for not doing what they're told. The Greek prime minister committed the ultimate sin of threatening to consult the people in a referendum, and he was removed so quick you can still see the dust settling. The Italian prime minister, a man with a barnacle-like ability to cling to office no matter what, was brushed aside like a piece of straw, and now both Italy and Greece are run by puppet governments that have been installed by a foreign power, and can no longer be regarded as sovereign nations by any honest measure of that term.

What part of the word "empire" do you people in Europe not understand?

The Italians were even told not to hold elections in the new year by an unelected bureaucrat who calls himself the President of the European Council, a man with the look and demeanour of a furtive rodent, Mr Anonymous from Belgium. Nobody knows who he is or where he came from, yet suddenly out of nowhere he's the emperor, I mean president of Europe. Not to be confused with the other emperor, the president of the European Commission, the thuggish closet Maoist, Mr Barroso. And I believe there's another president as well, some cipher from Luxembourg that nobody has ever heard of, and with good reason.

They're very fond of giving themselves grand titles to go with their massive salaries, these people. I'm surprised they haven't awarded each other a chest full of medals like the Soviet commissars they really are.

Predictably, they're using the crisis they created as an excuse to grab even more power for themselves. They've now demanded total control over every country's national budget. It seems the soft totalitarianism we had almost become used to in Europe is now openly hardening into a more familiar Soviet-style dictatorship which, people are belatedly realising, has been the goal all along.

Fortunately, there is still something, at least on a national level, that we can do about this democratically, and that's why there's been such a surge in support in several countries for freedom and independence parties who have come literally from nowhere in just a few short years, not least here in Britain, where the people have made it clear to the politicians that they demand a referendum on our continued membership of this outrageous political swindle, this federal dictatorship in the making.

Despite the fact that all three major parties have promised such a referendum, recently in Parliament they killed a debate on the subject when hundreds of MPs from all sides simply rolled over and voted the way they were told, because their poxy careers are more important to them than the wishes of the people who put them there. And, what's more, they fully expect to get away with it. They fully expect the people to go through the motions as usual at the next election and vote them straight back in.

But if they can't be trusted with the fundamentals, and they've shown with flying colours that they can't, what can they be trusted with?

It doesn't get any more fundamental than the right to decide how and by whom we are governed. Without that right we might as well have no rights at all.

So, wherever you stand in the political spectrum – left, right, red or blue, yellow, green or somewhere in between, this is something that should be uniting all of us, because it directly and profoundly affects all of us, and our children, in the most fundamental way.

If the fundamentals of a thing are wrong, it's likely that everything about it will be wrong, and will stay wrong. That's why we have to fix the fundamentals first and restore democracy before engaging in tribal politics, because frankly none of that stuff will have any substance anyway without the right of self-determination.

Nobody's political views are worth a damn without the means to have them implemented. Those means have been stolen from us by the very people to whom they were entrusted for safe keeping. Not just here in Britain, but in every European Union country where the political class have closed ranks against the people they purport to represent.

So, what are you going to do about this? How will you be voting next time around? Same again? Same as usual? If you do, you'll be guaranteeing that it's emperors all the way from here on in. And you'll also be enacting something of a political paradox – you'll be using your democratic franchise to vote against democracy, a bit like using one leg to kick the other from under you, because ultimately you will be voting against your own freedom, so you might as well be voting against water, or air.

107

The Intolerance of Diversity

December 22, 2011

I've just been reading a news report about some American atheists who have been trying to get a public Christmas nativity
scene removed because they say it makes them feel excluded
and intimidated and offended and blah blah blabbity-blah, boo
hoo hoo.

Can't you just feel the emotional trauma these poor people
must be suffering? No, me neither. Oddly, however, it is still
enough to make you weep.

This is what happens when atheism meets political correctness. I don't know if it has a name, but then it's so ugly it doesn't
really need one. And, as an atheist myself, I can't help but feel
horribly tainted by association. And believe me, I'm as atheist as
it's possible to be. I think religion is utter nonsense, and I claim
the right to criticise, ridicule and insult it as much as I like, but
not the right to stamp out harmless aspects of it, which is why
I'm a secularist, and not a totalitarian.

I have a copy of the Bible in my house because it's part of my cultural heritage, not because I think the Bible is true any more than I think Shakespeare's plays are true, but I wouldn't be without them either.

I like churches, especially the sound of church bells, and I don't want to see them bulldozed, but I do want to see the power of the Church not only bulldozed, but ground into a fine dust and buried in the deepest part of the deepest ocean on the furthest planet it's possible to find.

Religion needs to be kept in check when it tries to step on people or when it tries to elbow its way into their lives uninvited. The nativity doesn't do this. It doesn't even come close. It's part and parcel of the Christmas furniture. It's part and parcel of the culture that I, and most people in the western world, were born and raised in, and it only excludes people who want to be excluded.

It's not even as if it's a permanent fixture like, say, the Ten Commandments outside a court house. It will be gone in a couple of weeks.

And yes, we all know the story itself is ridiculous. The entire tableau is utterly barmy and worthy of open mockery and ridicule, but to claim that it sends a message of intimidation and exclusion and therefore must be banned is both infantile and sinister, and it simply isn't true. Yes, some people may choose to be offended, but some people are offended by anything, and frankly they can go to hell.

We get this crap every year, though. If it's not from atheists, it's from leftist academics or some other equality nazis who hate their own culture so much they can't wait to abolish it. This time last year I remember linking to a story which at the time I thought was the most outrageous piece of social manipulation I've seen for a while, where some idiots at a Canadian university... (Social psychologists, they call themselves. No, I don't know what it means either, so I looked it up and I'm still none the wiser, but I'd be willing to bet that if all the social psychologists on the planet were to disappear in a puff of smoke nobody would be worse off.) ... Anyway, these clowns concluded from their "scientific research" that Christmas trees should be removed from public places because they make non-Christians feel, guess what, excluded, and this inevitably damages their emotional wellbeing. Well, of course it does. How awful for them. And doubtless this also makes them feel terribly offended, not to mention intimidated and insulted and threatened, and let's not forget marginalised. Sounds like a fate worse than death, doesn't it?

Except that it's not true, because I'm a non-Christian – I couldn't be more non-Christian if I was from Mars – and I can tell you that I don't feel in the least bit excluded or intimidated or threatened or marginalised by Christmas trees or carol singers or nativity scenes or any other Christian aspect of a traditional Christmas. I expect to see these things in the public square where they belong. Indeed, I insist upon it. And if they're not there, if they've been removed because some self-righteous atheist fanatic or some finger-wagging diversity fascist has chosen to be offended and get the plug pulled, that's when I feel excluded and marginalised and intimidated and insulted and terribly terribly offended, and all this inevitably plays absolute havoc with my emotional wellbeing.

So please, militant atheists and cultural masochists alike,

please do me and everyone else a favour, leave Christmas alone for Christ's sake, and stop making fools of yourselves.

Peace, and a merry Christmas to everyone, but especially to Little Baby Jesus.

108

Tell the Truth about Islam

March 19, 2012

The Islamophobia industry is quick to whine and complain at every opportunity, as everybody knows, and lately they've been whining and complaining about what they call negative coverage of Islam in the British media, by which they mean truthful coverage – although, in truth, we don't get nearly enough of that.

For example, when it was revealed recently that there has been a large increase in so-called "honour" violence where Muslim women are brutalised and murdered by members of their own family, nowhere in the BBC report did it mention the one crucial ingredient – the religion of peace. This salient piece of information was carefully airbrushed out, as if to imply that this is a British phenomenon, as if society as a whole is to blame.

Similarly, we're always hearing about organised gangs of Muslim men exploiting and raping underage girls, yet the media never refer to these men by the religion whose misogynistic values have shaped their view of women, preferring instead to label them "Asians", which is a gross slander on Hindus and Sikhs who don't engage in this kind of behaviour, yet who are tarred with the same brush by cowardly and dishonest journalists afraid to offend the whining oversensitive professional victims of Islam.

People often say: "The bad things about Islam are cultural, not religious."

Really? What happens in Saudi Arabia isn't culture. It's pure religion. It's pure Islam, and it's pure insanity. We're talking about a country run with an iron fist by a handful of brutal conservative religious clerics. A country where they execute people for witchcraft, where they execute gay people and treat women as a subhuman species, and where gangs of fanatical scripture-sodden ignoramuses are allowed to roam the streets enforcing sharia with medieval rigour. The religion is the problem, not the culture.

The problem with Iran is the religion, not the culture. Iranians are not Arabs, but they've been conquered by an alien Arab religion, and now their country's entire focus is on an Arab situation, Palestine, not an Iranian one. This is because the religious fanatics who control Iran against the wishes of its people are insane. Their minds are so pickled by their barbaric religion, and they're so obsessed with killing Jews, they're determined to force a nuclear showdown. They're driven by powerful apocalyptic religious delusions which they intend to act upon the first chance they get. They're of the same mentality as the religious fanatics who controlled Europe hundreds of years ago, and if those people had had nuclear weapons, none of us would be here now.

Many of the Muslims here in Britain, including the gangs of child rapists (all of them), come from Pakistan, where the culture is shaped by the religion and blasphemy is a capital offence. It's what the religion demands, and the culture does what it's told, otherwise the religion will mobilise a mob of illiterate savages to riot in the streets, and scores, if not hundreds of people are likely to be killed. The religion is the problem, not the culture. The culture isn't great by any means, but without the religion it would be a damn sight better. And we in Britain are busy importing that religion wholesale into our society where it's about as welcome as the Norman invasion, despite all the platitudes and lies we hear from politicians about tolerance and respect and "community cohesion", because people have learned, as they've learned everywhere in the West, that this is far more than just a religion. It's an invasive political supremacist ideology that exploits religious freedom and cultural guilt to impose itself with constant demands for special treatment, always backed by the implicit threat of conflict and violence. In other words, through cultural terrorism.

So whether it's prayer rooms crowbarred into the workplace where they don't belong, Muslims allowed to pray in the street and block traffic, medical staff allowed to ignore hygiene rules, the police turning a blind eye to genital mutilation, universities letting jihadists recruit on campus, sharia courts dehumanising women, or the imposition of halal-only food on the entire population without their knowledge or consent, society, it seems, must always bow to the unreasonable demands of Islam, and anyone who dares to object is either vilified as a racist or openly threatened with violence.

This is what the media should be saying about Islam, if journalists had the guts to do their job and tell the truth, because it is the truth, and everybody knows it's the truth. And you can call me a racist for saying so if you want to, and a hate-monger and a bigot and all the rest of it – go through the card, be my guest – but when you finally run out of names it will still be the truth. Sorry about that.

Thanks to our moral cowardice, we now have hundreds of unregulated madrassas in Britain teaching tens of thousands of children to despise the culture they live in. That bodes well for the future of "community cohesion", doesn't it? A madrassa, in case you didn't know, is an Islamic school. In other words, it's the kind of place where you're likely to come out even more ignorant than when you went in.

And just last month we had a good example of the kind of mentality these places encourage when three Muslim men were convicted of stirring up hatred by passing out leaflets calling for gay people to be executed.

They pleaded guilty, by all accounts, but, to my mind, it would have been more accurate and more honest if they had pleaded insanity.

One of them said he did it because he wants to improve society. Well, there's a simple way for him to do that: emigrate, and take all his bigoted fuzzy-faced friends with him.

The prosecution argued that the leaflets were not educational when, in fact, they were extremely educational in that they plainly stated what Islam actually teaches and not what its mealy-mouthed apologists would like to pretend it teaches. Islam does call for the death penalty for homosexuality. It's a fact. And in countries where it's allowed to call the shots they enthusiastically carry it out.

Thanks to unwanted mass Islamic immigration, there are parts of Europe today where, if you make it known that you're gay (or Jewish, for that matter) you are virtually asking to be physically attacked. It's an indisputable fact that the more Muslims there are in a society (not Asians – Muslims) the less safe it's likely to be for gay people, or Jews, or women, or anyone attempting to exercise their fundamental right to freedom of speech.

So where exactly is all the positive coverage of this wretched religion supposed to come from? A religion that routinely responds to the slightest criticism by feigning a ludicrous knee-jerk sensitivity, when its own scripture is a handbook of insensitivity, brutality and social division. Slay the infidel wherever you find him. Execute gay people. Murder apostates. Subjugate women. Wipe out the Jews. Such an ideology has no claim on sensitivity, and the opinions of those who push it should be given less consideration than other people's, not more.

109

Israel and the United Nations

April 10, 2012

It isn't always easy to change your mind, especially when your opinions are based on emotion and not fact, but I'm encouraged to see that some people are beginning to change their mind about the situation the Middle East, despite the relentless anti-Israel coverage we're constantly force-fed by the western media, because, when people take the trouble to look at the facts they quickly realise that the Palestinian cause is insultingly bogus and phoney, that the terrorist Palestinian leadership are playing the free world like a Stradivarius, and that the whole problem could be solved peacefully and prosperously for everyone involved tomorrow if only they would stop murdering people and let it happen.

People also realise, when they look at the facts, that, for all the talk of an apartheid state in Israel, the only apartheid you'll find in the Middle East is in Arab countries who won't allow their Palestinians to integrate, denying them the most basic of human rights and condemning them to generations of misery and resentment because they need the refugee camps to remain permanently, festering like open sores, to gain sympathy from the gullible West and to con millions of good-hearted people here into supporting their religious war of hatred against Jews – all Jews. Indeed, the Hamas charter specifically calls for the killing of all Jews, just in case anyone was in any doubt.

However, although the tide of truth is beginning to turn, many people are still very critical of Israel's failure to abide by United Nations resolutions, especially to do with human rights. And yes, on the surface, that seems a legitimate concern. Assuming, of course, that a UN resolution is actually worth the paper it's written on. Let's pretend for the moment that it is, just for fun.

Yes, that's a real a puzzle, isn't it? Why would the Israelis ignore dozens of resolutions forced through by a cartel of anti-Semitic Bronze Age barbarians who would destroy their country and everyone in it, including women and children, given half a chance?

Beats me. I guess they must be fascists.

If you're one of the people who still think like this, let me try and explain to you why they do it, in case you are just too stubborn or too dense to figure it out for yourself.

The United Nations as it stands today is an embarrassing disgrace and an insult to humanity. Whatever moral authority it may once have had has been squandered. Its political corruption is matched only by its incompetence. (Just ask the people of Syria.) I wouldn't trust the United Nations to run a lemonade stand without thousands of people being needlessly killed.

Among its many failings, the United Nations encourages Islamic religious hatred and racism to dress itself up in the language of human rights, repeatedly allowing its Human Rights Council to be steamrollered in this regard by a cartel of fifty-seven mainly dictatorships and theocracies known as the Organization of Islamic... something or other. They keep changing it, and I can't be bothered to keep up. I don't really care what they call themselves. It's enough to know what they are, and that's brutal barbaric Islamic hellholes that nobody in their right mind would choose to live in and whose own human rights records are not only worse than Israel's, but immeasurably worse.

Countries like Iran, where they execute children; Sudan, where they practise slavery and casual genocide; Pakistan, which is supposed to be a democracy, but which is actually a dictatorship of religious ignorance, violence and fear, and where every year a thousand women are murdered by members of their own family; and of course Saudi Arabia, the black hole of Islamic barbarism, the world's leading source of terrorist funding, and the absolute moral anus of the universe.

These are some of the countries behind the blizzard of resolutions directed at Israel. Countries that belong on the moral high ground like a rattlesnake belongs in a lunchbox. Countries united by a virulent religious hatred of Jews for being Jews. These are the loudest voices at the United Nations, so of course the Israelis ignore them. It would be suicidal not to.

When it comes to Israel, the United Nations is a crooked court with a jury full of hanging judges. It doesn't get any more corrupt than that. And frankly, I'm baffled as to why the Americans still tolerate this disgusting travesty on their soil and pay all its bills. They should kick it out of the country and tell it to relocate to Tehran or Islamabad where the organisation of Islamic fascists can go ahead and pass all the fancy resolutions they like, all written out in the most beautiful Arabic, and then promptly shove them where the sun don't shine.

In attacking Israel over and over, while ignoring the real human rights violators – not only the Islamic barbarians, but the North Koreas and Burmas of this world – the United Nations has shown itself to be nakedly partisan and to be effectively an enemy of Israel. And as I see it, unless you're an idiot, or a western liberal, you don't take orders from your enemies.

110

Hello Saudi Arabia

May 2, 2012

I've had a few emails recently from people in Saudi Arabia who seem genuinely puzzled about why I criticise their country; a country, let's remind ourselves, that's actively funding the spread of Islamic extremism throughout the West like a poison dye; that's exporting millions of textbooks around the world teaching children supremacism, separatism and hatred of non-Muslims; a country that donates tens of millions of dollars a year to schools in Pakistan that train children to be suicide bombers; a country where women enjoy a status somewhere between human beings and livestock, and where people are executed for things that are not even crimes in the civilised world; and a country whose ruling class indulge themselves freely in alcohol, drugs and every other vice you can think of while condemning their people to a social and psychological prison for their own moral good.

And they really have to ask?

One guy said: "I'm from Saudi Arabia, and I'm proud of my country."

Well, good for you, but forgive me for asking why. If you live in Saudi Arabia what on earth have you got to be proud of? If you couldn't dig money straight out of the ground you'd all be starving. The only thing your country has to offer the world is oil. Well, it's not the only thing, but we don't need any sand, and we're all up to here with jihad, thanks very much. Your country, like the whole Arab world, is entirely and pathetically dependent on western technology, much of it Israeli, without which it couldn't function. What the hell have you got to be proud of?

Maybe you're proud of the fact that your country leads the world in public executions for things like sorcery. We went through that in Europe hundreds of years ago, and we're still embarrassed about it. How do you expect us to feel watching you repeat the same insanity? And there is no other word for it. It's not culturally different, it's not conservative. It's insane. And it's insane because your country is run by insane people, a small group of hardcore ultra-conservative religious clerics, each the proud holder of a PhD in pious ignorance, who call themselves the Supreme Council of Islamic Scholars.

That sounds like a real brainfest, doesn't it? Actually no, you're right, it sounds like a bunch of rancid old closet homosexuals digging around in scripture to find ways of justifying their infantile fear of women. Men who have reduced their spiritual focus to such a dry ordeal of repression and vindictive cruelty they've sucked all the life out of it and out of themselves.

And they're always looking for new ways to embarrass their country in the eyes of history, to cement its reputation as a backwater of superstition and ignorance, and to ensure that their ugly and poisonous Wahhabi doctrine will be derided and ridiculed by the whole world, now and for many centuries to come.

Recently they instructed the religious police (yes, religious police) to prevent anyone who even looks as if they might be gay from entering a school or a university.

They really seem to have an major problem with gay people, these guys. It's almost as big as the problem they have with women, and that's the psychological equivalent of a two hundred pound tumour that has to be pushed around in a wheelbarrow.

Indeed, they're so obsessed with homosexuality you can't help but be suspicious. When they condemn it as forcefully as any closet gay Christian televangelist who consorts with rent boys, what are we supposed to think?

And no absurdity is too great, either, for the paranoid imagination of the Saudi religious "scholar", like the recent pronouncement that allowing women to drive cars will turn everybody in the country gay because there won't be any virgins left.

Well, apart from the faulty logic, I think they're way behind the curve on that one. It's well known that homosexuality is absolutely rampant in Saudi Arabia, despite being a capital offence, and it's almost impossible to find a Saudi man (and that would include clerics) who has not had a gay experience, because women are just so hermetically inaccessible.

And who can be surprised? If you insist on keeping men and women apart in such an unnatural way you have to be prepared for the natural consequence – a rise in homosexual activity. Living in a crazy kingdom doesn't make anybody less human, and certain biological urges will be satisfied one way or another.

Of course there is absolutely nothing wrong with being gay.

The ancient Greeks were gay, and there was nothing wrong with them. They routinely had sex with other men, just as they do today in Saudi Arabia, and there's nothing wrong with it there either. Which is just as well, because it's no secret, boys, so you can step out of that closet any time you like.

All over the world Saudi Arabia has long had a reputation as a gay country, a country with one king and millions of queens, and the only people who don't seem to know it are the Saudis. Well, now you do. Indeed there's a very good chance that, by percentage of population, Saudi Arabia is actually the gay capital of the world. Now there's something you can be proud of.

Of course you Saudis wouldn't be in this ludicrous and embarrassing situation in the first place if you had the basic decency to treat women as human beings and not as possessions.

And when you say to me: "We treat our women well. Our women are looked after and protected, not like yours. Don't tell us how to treat our women. Look after your own...", that's the whole point, geniuses, they're not your women. You have no ownership. You have no jurisdiction. All you have is brute force. And if that's all you can use (and it is) you have no business calling yourselves men. I wish there was a nicer way to say that, but there isn't.

And let me tell you, I'm not saying any of this to be insulting, because, believe it or not, I don't need any more enemies. It's just that sometimes the truth can sound like an insult when you're not used to hearing it. But the good news is, thanks to the internet and western technology, you soon will be.

111

Can I Say This?

May 27, 2012

Well, we've been enjoying quite a heatwave here in London for the last week or so, and the last thing I wanted to do was make a video. I certainly didn't expect to be talking about Saudi Arabia again so quickly, but my last video about that country being a gay volcano on the brink of eruption got quite a heated response from a few people there, including violent threats and other abuse. I guess it must have touched a nerve – a big old gay nerve. And I suppose that's understandable. Anyone who lives in a country where they execute gay people is bound to get a little jumpy when somebody rattles the closet door.

And believe me, boys, I sympathise. This is why I've always thought it was a great idea to put a gay bar next to the proposed Ground Zero mosque in New York, if it ever gets built. Then when Saudi clerics go over there to preach violent jihad they can drop in next door and dip their wick between hate sermons. Of course they'll need to have a private door installed between the two buildings so that they can maintain their religious and cultural integrity by doing it, as usual, in secret.

Although Saudi Arabia has a worldwide reputation as a gay country, they do execute gay people there, so you wouldn't expect too many of them to be coaxed out of the closet, no matter how many millions may be crammed in there, at least not until they'd had a clear lead from somebody with absolute religious authority, like the Grand Mufti perhaps, or one of his boyfriends.

If one of those guys was honest enough to come out as gay, to acknowledge the culture that actually exists (and not the fantasy one they want us to believe exists), I bet the floodgates would open and they'd all be at it.

Even the religious police wouldn't interfere. They'd be too busy sewing their costumes for the Mecca pride parade (Muslims only, of course). You see, many of those guys have done time in prison, so they're happy to keep the sexes apart. They just can't keep their hands off each other.

But look, I don't want to overdo this whole Saudi gay thing here. It's good for a few laughs up to a point, but there are plenty of worse things about Saudi Arabia than sexual hypocrisy. Like the untold billions they're pumping into worldwide jihad, for example, funding hardline madrassas and hate-preaching mosques and creeping sharia throughout the western world.

Also, the Americans tell us that the Saudi Arabians are the world's leading source of terrorist funding.

And this is because, although we in the West are not at war with Islam, Wahhabi Islam (the batshit crazy one with all the money) is very much at war with us, only we're too stupid to see it.

It's a war of attrition that they intend to win by taking full advantage of the thing they most despise and would abolish if they could: freedom of religion.

Don't bother being a Christian in Saudi Arabia. Your religion is against the law there. And, if you're stupid enough to start preaching it, you could be executed, in public

Meanwhile, thousands of Saudi-funded mosques are being built all over the free world. And even when they're publicly shown to be preaching misogyny, homophobia, anti-Semitism and violence, nothing is ever done about it because that might cause offence. Indeed, here in Britain, the people who report it are more likely to be arrested as criminals.

Also, as most people know by now, the Saudi regime is a leading light in the Islamic campaign to stamp out free speech at the United Nations and introduce a worldwide blasphemy law. However, after decades of Islamic phoney grievance-mongering, not to mention the cowardly connivance of western politicians eager to pass laws that silence their own citizens, people in the West are finally waking up to just how essential free speech is to our survival as a free society, and also to the realisation that this is precisely why the Islamic dictatorships are attacking it. It's not because they're offended about anything, believe me. They're not that sensitive.

They're doing it because they know that, if they can neutralise free speech, the guts will have been ripped out of western civilisation and our society will rot and decay from within. Indeed, the process is already visibly under way in several European countries where people have been prosecuted as criminals for holding legitimate non-violent opinions and for telling the truth.

And this is why every freedom-loving person in the West should be absolutely determined that the Islamic war on free speech will never, ever be allowed to succeed, not by one inch, not at any price, not now, and not in a million years. Not even in the length of time it would take for the entire country of Saudi Arabia to pass, sand grain by sand grain, through an egg timer – which is all it will be fit for when we find an alternative to oil (and stop the oil companies from sabotaging it), and many of us here in the free world (that's the civilised world to you boys in Saudi) are hoping that day arrives very soon indeed.

Free speech means being able to express an honest opinion (in case you didn't know) and my honest opinion is that Wahhabi Islam is such an obvious mental affliction that science ought to be looking for a cure. It's a truly horrible, heartless and cruel ideology that despises humankind (especially the female half) and I believe its presence on this planet is a stain on all humanity. And when it finally passes, as one day it surely must, because nothing that unnatural and inhuman could possibly last forever, its memory will linger like a bad smell, as a warning for generations to come. Like a ghostly gibbet by the roadside of history, a bony finger of death beckoning us back to a more brutal and primitive past, it will serve as a grim reminder of what happens to human beings when religion is allowed to go too far.

112

Waiting for Jesus

July 12, 2012

I know Christianity is not a violent death cult, unlike some we could name (well, not any more, anyway), but it certainly does some strange things to people's minds. Like the idiot in West Virginia who died recently from a rattlesnake bite because he thought Jesus wanted him to handle serpents.

He got the idea of handling poisonous snakes from his father. Guess what happened to his father.

Stupid or insane? You decide. Although I think a strong case could be made for both. Or maybe it's just nature's way of cleaning up after itself. Evolution in action before our very eyes.

Every Easter in the Philippines there are people who have themselves nailed to crosses so that they can know the suffering of Jesus. I reckon if Jesus is up there looking down at those people on their crosses, or at the people with rattlesnakes, he'll still be suffering. He'll be shaking his head and wondering why the hell he ever bothered, especially when he looks around the world and sees millions worshipping him as a god like a bunch of savages when they know full well it's not what he preached and it's the last thing he wants. He must tear his hair in frustration whenever some imbecile prays to the graven idol of his crucified image like some juju doll. Or maybe he just laughs. What else can you do?

Either way, I wish he'd come back and do something about it, because it's getting embarrassing, and besides, there's something I'd like to ask him.

He's supposed to come back anyway at some point to redeem the righteous, of course, and to vanquish the Antichrist, along with any Jews who refuse to convert to Christianity. So presumably he'll have to vanquish himself, unless he agrees to convert and start worshipping himself. Could get complicated.

I hope he turns up, though, not just for my sake, but for the sake of all those righteous folks who have their heart set on having their soul saved. They'll be so disappointed if he doesn't make it, especially when they start thinking about all that money they've been tithing into the bank accounts of the multi-millionaires who run Christianity. That might be almost enough to make a person lose faith, and put down their rattlesnake.

Also, of course, if he doesn't turn up it will mean that the last two thousand years of brutal superstitious Christian persecution were all for nothing, and what a shame it would be to waste all that self-destructive misery and guilt. After all, it has helped to make us who we are.

I wonder how Jesus will arrive. Do you think he'll come in a style befitting his glorious majesty, bursting through the clouds in a fiery chariot, slaughtering unbelievers and heretics, scything them down like ripe corn, as many believers hope and pray, or will he come on the bus?

The short answer is we just don't know. Even after centuries of abstruse and pointless speculation it remains one of the great theological mysteries.

One thing is for sure, though, if he turns up he'll be very popular. I wouldn't mind betting he'll be so popular he'll have to ride around inside a bulletproof glass box surrounded by body-guards. Twelve of them, I reckon. Eleven good and one evil is my guess.

What I'd like to know is how we're supposed to recognise Jesus when he arrives, because nobody actually knows what he looks like. Everyone seems to have created him in their own image, so if you put all the different versions of Jesus togeth-er you'd end up with some kind of Middle Eastern Oriental Anglo-Saxon blue-eyed black man. No wonder he was a one off. That's some special DNA, isn't it? But then that's Jesus for you. We know he was special. He was never just an ordinary human being. Yes, he was flesh and blood, but only as far as necessary for divinity to dip itself temporarily into the human mud pool. You want proof? He was born to a virgin. How much more proof do you need? The rest of us can only dream of being born to virgins, but to Jesus it was second nature, because he's so special. Everything about him was special. Everything he did was a miracle. He was such a superhero I'm surprised he didn't fly around wearing a cape with a big J on it.

And of course this is precisely how we'll recognise Jesus, when he actually does some of the superhero stuff we've been led to expect. This is not a gig for an imposter, after all. He needs to actually take on the Antichrist and give him a comprehensive spanking. That's not the kind of thing you can bluff. You've either got it or you haven't. And we know he has it because we know that, when faced with adversity, he can usually produce a miracle from his back pocket. It's the miracles that make him special, isn't that right?

I wonder if Jesus will do a few miracles to entertain the crowd while he's waiting for the Antichrist to show his cowardly face. Of course he will, because he knows that's what people are really there for. He knows that if not for the miracles Christians wouldn't give him or his message the time of day. He knows that Christians need miracles because they don't have the wisdom or the moral backbone to follow his teachings without the goddamned miracles. So yes, he'll probably open a box of snakes or something to keep everybody happy.

But the reason I'm looking forward to Jesus coming back is because I want to ask him why he disappeared so quickly after the resurrection without giving people a chance to verify it. He must have known the uncertainty that would cause, and the centuries of righteous bloodletting that would inevitably ensue, which makes me wonder just how divine and godly this character really was.

After all, he wasn't so shy about all the other miracles, was he? When it came to walking on water or feeding a multitude it was: "Look at me, look at me, the lamb of God is in the house..."

Yet his final and greatest miracle, the only miracle that really matters, is the one miracle nobody saw. Am I the only one who smells a rat here?

Rising from the dead and ascending bodily into heaven; such a momentous event. Surely that should have been a special occasion witnessed by at least a multitude – that's got to be minimum.

Yet what happens? He disappears like a fugitive, like a thief in the night, skulking away as if he's got something to hide. Well, I think it stinks. And doubly so, because it's been the direct cause of so much persecution and misery on this earth over the last two thousand years, all of it unnecessary, and all of it his fault.

So this is why I'm looking forward to his imminent and glorious return, because I would like to buttonhole Jesus and ask him directly if he's really working for Satan – just to see what he says.

113

American Dhimmi

July 20, 2012

Some people didn't like my last video very much. They told me I should be attacking Islam, not Christianity. Why didn't someone tell me sooner? All the videos I've made and not once have I attacked Islam. What was I thinking about?

(I blame the Jews, don't you?)

Well, in this video I intend to say a few words in support of Christians, but I still think Christianity is a laughable raft of insulting nonsense that any intelligent six-year-old child would dismiss out of hand if they were allowed to have a mind of their own.

I'm referring specifically to Christians in the Muslim world, God help them – if you'll pardon the expression.

Who would have predicted that the Arab Spring, that bright new tomorrow of yesterday, would so quickly degenerate into a sordid Muslim Brotherhood takeover with people arrested for blasphemy, women harassed in the street, and the violent persecution of Christians?

Actually, I would have predicted it. Oh, you as well? And everybody you know? Well, it wasn't that hard to see coming down the road, was it?

What a waste of a revolution. They finally get democracy and they vote for a bunch of religious fanatics. People that stupid don't deserve to be free.

I guess somewhere down the line they'll have to go through the whole thing all over again. Only next time I hope they'll be able to resist the urge to gang rape female news reporters in the street, although I wouldn't bet on it.

The so-called Arab Spring has been a winter of persecution for Christians in particular, who are being driven out as sharia is driven in. Like the Jews before them, Christians are being ethnically cleansed from Muslim countries, but the western media don't want to talk about it because it means having to focus on the hateful supremacist doctrine of Islam, an ideology that confers inferior status on non-believers and demands their submission as dhimmis.

Those noble Egyptian soldiers who refused to fire on their Muslim brothers during the revolution had no such qualms about shooting unarmed Christians in the street for protesting against unprovoked Muslim violence.

Such is the insanity that even in Syria, despite being murdered in their thousands by their own government, the rebels have found time to put Christians on notice to leave.

I'm no fan of Christianity, but I am a fan of civilisation and justice, and both of those things seem to be in very short supply in a part of the world where Christianity is being systematically erased, while the Christian president of the United States says nothing and looks the other way for fear of causing offence. He is a Christian, isn't he?

I know some people think Obama is a Muslim because his middle name is Hussein, because he bowed to the Saudi King like a vassal, because he sucks up to Islam every chance he gets, because he humiliated his country by apologising to Islamic terrorists, and because his administration is crippled by a chronic political correctness that empowers jihadis pretending to be Americans, but I wouldn't say that makes the president a Muslim. I'd say it makes him a dhimmi. And I think he and his administration are doing their best to turn the United States into a dhimmi nation.

Recently he welcomed the election of an Islamist president in Egypt; a man who, during his campaign (a campaign supported by the US government) made the statement: "The Koran is our constitution, the Prophet is our leader, jihad is our path, and death in the name of Allah is our goal." A man who belongs to an organisation that has vowed in its charter to infiltrate western society and destroy it from within. In short, the new Egyptian president is a jihadi, which is a word Obama's administration can't even bring itself to use in case somebody gets offended.

It's actually quite amusing to watch an American government spokesman wriggling around trying not to say the words "Islamic" or "jihad" when talking about Islamic jihad until you realise the level of denial you're actually witnessing, and you can't help but wonder if it's possible to trust this person's judgment or their word about anything at all.

Oh, and you might like to know that, despite the First Amendment, the Obama administration is behaving on the world stage as if free speech is actually negotiable. Right now they're engaged in dialogue with a bunch of Islamic dictatorships to help them find ways of curbing free speech through the United Nations Human Rights Council, when what passes for human rights in any of those places would be against the law in the civilised world, and the only dialogue any of them deserve is three short words: Go to hell. Oh, and p.s. Stop murdering Christians.

Obama wants to be cosy with Islam because he's got an Islamic background himself and because he wants to be cosy with the Third World in general. He isn't just America's first black president, he's America's first Third World president, and that's his problem.

There must be a part of Obama that feels so guilty about going to America, becoming successful, and leaving all those people behind that he just has to reach out and say: "Hey people, it's me, Barry. You still like me, don't you?"

But they don't like him, because they despise weakness, especially in the Islamic world, and he's even less popular there than George W. Bush, which is something I'd have thought a person would have to work at, but Obama has managed it effortlessly.

And he's getting less popular in the First World as well, because people can see how he deals with Islamic extremists, and they can see that he's not actually fit to be president of the United States.

Don't get me wrong, he might be to fit to lead another country, a European country perhaps, where fundamental rights are not quite so important. Besides, he is a European by instinct, anyway; an accommodationist, a compromiser, a dhimmi.

He doesn't realise that the American president has a duty beyond America to the whole free world to stand up for American values, not Third World values, because despite all the propaganda they are not, in fact, equal.

If Christians are being persecuted in the Muslim world purely because of their religion – and they are – the American president has a duty to speak out, loudly and often until somebody listens. Instead this president chooses to remain silent. He chooses to continue shovelling bucketloads of American taxpayers' money into the Arab world without even a polite request that they stop murdering Christians.

And if you think that's slimy, every year the US State Department issues a report on the state of human rights in all UN member countries. This year for the first time they removed the section on religious freedom, thus neatly sidestepping the need to acknowledge the violent persecution of Christians since the glorious revolution for freedom and democracy.

Who would have thought the United States, of all countries, would so cravenly turn its back on persecuted Christians in their darkest hour just so as not to offend their Muslim persecutors?

America, thanks to this president, is already a dhimmi nation.

114

The Ugliest Newspaper in Britain

August 1, 2012

Here in Britain we have a newspaper called the *Guardian*, whose reputation as a sanctimonious mouthpiece for the great multicultural con trick is now being eclipsed by a more rancid reputation for anti-Semitism.

The *Guardian* used to represent what used to be called the liberal tradition, and at one time it could be relied on for reasonably balanced coverage; sloping to the left, of course, but in a fair way, an honest way. Those days have gone.

Nowadays the *Guardian* has become so obsessed with the state of Israel, and has come to hate it with such a lopsided Scandinavian intensity, that it has lost all sense of proportion.

Nowadays the *Guardian* publishes writers who engage in anti-Semitic slurs, it willingly acts as a propaganda platform for the murdering terrorists of Hamas, and it misrepresents the facts in the Middle East to persuade its readers to support a fascist religious war of hate against a genuine democracy where Arabs and Jews have equal rights – although you'll never hear about that in the *Guardian*, whose writers prefer to push the lie, the fiction, of the apartheid state.

When it was forced to respond to repeated accusations of being anti-Semitic the *Guardian* seemed a lot more concerned with possible damage to its reputation than with whether or not anti-Semitism is a bad thing, when I think we all know that if Muslims were complaining about Islamophobia they'd be trampling over each other at the *Guardian* to put things right. But Jews? Meh.

And what all this means is that if you let it be known that you read the *Guardian* it now says something about you that, on reflection, you may not want it to say. In short, the *Guardian* is now stigmatising its own readers – not that many of them don't do a fine job of stigmatising themselves.

Guardian readers are, in the main, educated middle-class people who regard themselves as liberal, leftish intellectual types. (Not the common clay, as it were.) And many of them inhabit a rarefied bubble of hypocrisy that only they seem unaware of. For example, they call themselves liberal, yet they're often the most enthusiastic about censoring the opinions of others, which is about the most illiberal thing you can do.

This is because the *Guardian* is written by and for the same narrow class of patronising know-it-all pinheads who have stolen the BBC from the rest of us and destroyed its impartiality. The kind of people who are so smug in their shallow certainties, so sure of the moral superiority of their views, that they have no compunction about slandering anyone who disagrees as a fascist or a crank.

Such is the BBC's hatred of Israel, by the way, that they

couldn't even give it a capital city in their Olympic guide. Yet they gave one to the Palestinians who haven't even got a country, and never will have, the way they're going about it.

Both the *Guardian* and the BBC are part of what's called the "progressive consensus" under whose auspices the language has been systematically emasculated, and words like "tolerance", "fairness", "diversity" and "progressive" no longer mean what they say. In each case the shell of the word is still there, but it's been hollowed out and filled with something altogether less savoury and actually quite sinister.

In this artificial PC newspeak world, the feckless and stupid, for example, are never referred to as feckless or stupid because that might damage their self-esteem. Instead they're called disadvantaged and vulnerable, which renders them victims, and, as such, automatically virtuous. And we all know by now that the golden rule for virtuous victims is that they should never be required to take responsibility for their actions or their circumstances. It must always, somehow, be somebody else's fault. It's what I call the Palestinian syndrome, and it saturates the *Guardian* from cover to cover.

So who reads the *Guardian*? Multiculties, liberal lefties, touchy-feely bleeding hearts. (Is that a stereotype? I do hope not.) The kind of people who cause ten times as many problems as they solve because they're so wilfully naive on everyone else's behalf. People who throw the words "racist" and "Islamophobe" around like monkeys with their own faeces, and who love diversity but make sure their own kids go to a school where everybody speaks English.

Maybe you know some fossilised old lefty who's still mentally wearing a Che Guevara T-shirt; you can bet your life they read the *Guardian*. And you probably know one of those comically self-righteous anti-capitalists with a mortgage and a pension; there's another *Guardian* reader. Self-hating Jews who support the Palestinians, women and gay people who defend Islamic misogyny and homophobia all read the *Guardian*. And you know you're firmly in *Guardian* territory when you find yourself being lectured on social justice by some middle-aged university-educated prick who has spent his whole life on the dole.

Guardian readers are the kind of people who gravitate to the high moral ground on just about every issue, because their values, being leftish liberal values, are automatically more virtuous than everybody else's. So virtuous are they, in fact, that they appear to be impregnable even to the stigma of anti-Semitism if it's in a good cause. And there is no better cause for a committed Guardianista, no cause more holy (meaning more fashionable to support at dinner parties) than romanticising the murdering terrorists of Hamas as freedom fighters, when freedom is actually what they're fighting against.

The *Guardian* and its sheeplike readers agonise endlessly about the poor Palestinians, while maintaining a rigorous ideological blindness to the core problem, which is that the Jews want peace and the Arabs don't because the Arabs are driven primarily by religious hatred. So whatever the Jews concede will never, ever be enough, because the Arabs want blood. They want the Jews dead. They don't want a two-state solution, *Guardian* readers, they want a one-state solution with no goddamned Jews in it, and they've repeatedly made it crystal clear that they'll settle for nothing less. Is everybody deaf?

So, if this is your position (and if you support Hamas, as the *Guardian* does, it is definitely your position – *sieg heil*, anyone?) then you need to be a bit more honest about your position and admit that what you're supporting, ultimately, is religious genocide.

On the other hand, if it's not your position, then maybe you should do yourself a favour and stop reading the *Guardian*, because right now every time you pick that thing up you leave a film of filth on your soul.

115

The Crisis of Secularism

August 30, 2012

When senior clergymen have nothing better to do, which is all the time, they love to complain about the threat of secularism, which they usually depict as barbarism on a stick, essentially; a kind of dark atheist totalitarian nightmare where religion has been stamped out and we've all reverted to a kind of amoral hedonistic savagery.

Well, whatever that may be, and however attractive it may sound to some people, that is not secularism.

Secularism doesn't mean no religion. It means religion for those who want it and no religion for those who don't. It means freedom of religion and freedom from religion in equal measure for a change. It means less unearned power, privilege and influence for the political organisation of religion and the people who make their living from it, but not for anybody else.

So naturally clergy regard it as the work of Satan, as do evangelical leaders, according to a poll from last summer. Although many ordinary Christians are rightly worried about the spread of Islam, their leaders, the ones who make a living from their religion, regard secularism as a greater threat. Of course they do. (Send money now, by the way, in Jesus' name.)

Recently an American Christian judge made the extraordinary claim that secularism leads to sharia law, which is a bit like saying that penicillin causes infection.

American judges are not known to be the brightest bulbs on the Christmas tree at the best of times, so we can probably give this guy the benefit of the doubt and assume that he was confusing secularism with multiculti dhimmitude. You see, a person who opposes Christianity but who appeases and enables Islam is not a secularist. The word for such a person is a dhimmi. (Well, there are other words, but I want to keep the language in this video as clean as I can so that the whole family can enjoy it.)

In fact, secularism is the only way to guarantee that sharia law can never get a foothold, so Christians, if they had any sense, would be lobbying for it and voting for it in droves. If they had any sense.

The truth is that secularism is under threat today in a way it hasn't been for many years, thanks partly to the uncompromising nature of the religion of permanent offence, and also thanks to our ridiculous culture of accommodation and unwarranted respect for religious belief, which Christian leaders are exploiting to the max, of course, because they are politicians first and foremost.

They don't seem to care that, in misrepresenting secularism for their own selfish ends, they're aiding and abetting the most virulent and dangerous form of religion on the planet, political

Islam. Unlike the fantasy sin of denying the holy spirit, that's a sin that really is unforgivable, because Islam has only been a prominent feature of western life for a couple of decades or so, yet in that short time it has managed to eat into our basic civil liberties with constant demands for special treatment always backed up by the implicit threat of violence. As a consequence, our diet has been adulterated with the barbarism of halal, we have sharia courts here in the UK where women are treated as less than human, and all over the western world we've been saddled with repressive hate speech laws that are more dangerous than the opinions they criminalise, all in the name of not offending Islam.

Wherever this religion goes in the world there's intolerance and there's conflict and people become less free. The evidence is right there for us. We have no excuse. It's happening before our very eyes in the wake of the so-called Arab Spring. Surely it's obvious that only a rigorously secular society is capable of keeping Islam at bay.

Well not, apparently, to Christian clergy who carry on blithely spreading their lies and depicting secularism as the epitome of evil, none more assiduously than the Pope of Rome, who claims that secularism has left deep scars on traditionally Christian countries. Really? I bet they're nowhere near as deep as the scars the Catholic Church has left. He shouldn't be so modest.

He says humankind is groping in the dark, unable to distinguish between good and evil, when over the last few years we've had ample evidence that it's the Catholic Church and the men who run it who are unable to distinguish good from evil.

This pope presided over years of child rape by Catholic priests and did nothing about it, then stonewalled the issue when it confronted him. Every concession has had to be dragged out of him. The fact that some people still regard him as a source of moral authority is frankly perverse. It's as if OJ Simpson ran for US president, and won in a landslide.

Yet this wretched man has the nerve to depict secularism as somehow immoral. To him, the only thing worse than a secularist is a secularist wearing a condom. He has even gone to the trouble of setting up a whole new evangelical unit within the Vatican to combat what he calls "the crisis of secularism". That's right, the crisis of religious freedom, the freedom of everyone to believe whatever they like and to worship whatever they like, but not to impose it on others, which, again, is what secularism actually means. And the Pope is against this, which shows that he knows better than Jesus, because if we all took the advice of Jesus to keep your religion to yourself and seek the kingdom of heaven within, we would automatically have a secular society, because we would have no need for the political organisation of religion or the professional parasites we know as clergy. They are the only people in any way threatened by secularism, and that's why they're the ones who are always bleating about it.

116

Your Moral Guide

September 11, 2012

Religious people often say that atheists have no morals because they have no moral guide. If you believe this, let me ask you something. If you're a Christian, chances are the Bible is your moral guide, but is that all of the Bible, or just some of it?

It's just the good bits, isn't it? The bits you've cherry-picked because obviously if you wanted to live in a Leviticus-style society where people are stoned and mutilated for insane and trivial reasons you could simply move to Iran.

But how do you decide which are the good bits and which are the bad in the Bible? What do you use as a moral guide? The Bible? Surely not. If so, you'd simply accept the bad along with the good, which is clearly what the Bible wants you to do, otherwise the bad wouldn't be there in the first place, would it?

But no, you don't do that. You defy the Bible. You sift out the bad and discard it for the ignorant primitive barbarism it is. In short, you edit the Bible to suit your own sensibilities. So where do you get the moral guidance to impose your authority on the word of the Bible?

It has to come from a higher source, doesn't it? (These things usually do.) And it does, of course. It comes from you. You are a higher source than the Bible, a much higher source. The criminals who run religion don't want you to know or to act upon this because then their influence over you would be zero, yet the evidence is clear. You sifted the good from the bad in the Bible without the Bible's help, you did it against the Bible's will, and you did it all on your own, because, whether you like it or not, you've got a conscience, which means that you are capable of distinguishing good from evil without the help of scripture, and you've just proven it beyond any shadow of doubt.

So, in fact the Bible is not your moral guide. You are. It doesn't provide you with a moral compass. You do. And the only faith you need is faith in yourself. O happy day.

117

A Word to Rioting Muslims

September 20, 2012

Well, once again we see multiple violent tantrums from the religion of permanent offence. Some things never change, do they? Once again we see Islam self-detonate (if you'll pardon the expression) and show once again why it's about as welcome on this planet as an asteroid. Once again we see thousands of Islamic nutcases take time out from beating up their wives to show their sensitive side. How? By smashing up the towns they live in, egged on by clerical ignoramuses whose motives are even lower than the literacy level of their followers. And once again we in the civilised world are being urged to censor ourselves out of respect for a religion that violates the human rights of half the people on the planet, and that doubles as a political ideology indistinguishable from Nazism.

It would be funny if it wasn't so obscene. Or should that be the other way round?

To call these riots infantile and imbecilic is to give them a dignity they don't deserve. They can only be described as Islamic.

Let me get this straight. We're supposed to show tolerance and respect for a religion that doesn't know the meaning of either word, and goes out of its way to prove it every day? We're supposed to amend our values to accommodate a religion that accommodates nothing and nobody? Dream on, people. It's not going to happen, because with Islam it's always a one-way street. We've learned that lesson the hard way. We can't afford any more tolerance and respect. We've been sucked dry. And we've become weary of manufactured Islamic grievance. It's such a bore that now when we hear some bearded buffoon or some bag-headed bimbo telling us how offended they are, we can't even be bothered to laugh any more. Not even when the Turkish prime minister hilariously demands that Islamophobia now be recognised as a crime against humanity, when, given its track record, there's a much stronger case for making Islam a crime against humanity. (Besides, Turkey is already hypocritically guilty of one of the greatest crimes against humanity in history, the Armenian genocide, a crime it doesn't even have the balls to admit to.)

When Muslims start showing the same level of outrage about things that are genuinely offensive, like the thousands of women and girls who are murdered, mutilated and raped every year in their countries, then we might start taking them a bit more seriously. As it is, there is nothing on this planet less deserving of sympathy or respect than Muslim outrage. Indeed, there's something deeply comical about it. It's so contrived and so cringingly un-self-aware it's impossible to take seriously, even if we wanted to. And nobody in their right mind wants to any more.

There was a time when Islam was given the benefit of the doubt by many people in the West. Now we think it's poison and we wish we had never heard of it, because twenty years of baseless grievance-mongering and knee-jerk offence have shown us this religion for what it really is, and now we don't like it, we don't trust it, and we are never going to respect it – and we don't care how Muslims feel about that.

Everything is an insult to this religion. Everything causes offence. Well, nobody gives a damn any more, people. You've done it to death. You've killed the goose that laid the golden egg. So now, if you're an offended Muslim, go and stick your head in the oven for all we care.

And if you think that if you keep up the violence the West will eventually cave in, it's not going to happen. Even if the politicians want it to, the people won't allow it. We'll carry on speaking our minds openly and freely, because it's our birth-right, and it can't be taken away from us. It can only be given away. And we are giving Islam nothing, because Islam gives us nothing. It's a religion permanently on the take. Gimme gimme gimme is all we ever hear. "Give me respect, even though I haven't earned it. Give me special treatment, or I'll be offended and you'll be a racist."

Well, we're sick and tired of hearing it, we're sick and tired of Islam, and we're sick and tired of the needless conflict and intimidation that comes from this religion at every turn.

All week we've heard Muslims telling us that we in the West need to understand how important the Prophet is to them. We do understand it, and we don't care. That's the point. We don't care now, and we are never going to care. Get used to it.

We don't give a damn about your feelings. Our feelings are more important. And our feelings tell us that we're sick to the back teeth of hearing about your religion, so stick a sock in it.

And no amount of violence is going to change a thing. The more you riot and scream and shout the less we're going to listen. It will simply stiffen our resolve not to be bullied and pushed around by people whose values we don't respect because you've given us no reason to respect them, and, more to the point, because you're incapable of giving us such a reason.

In short, we will not be told what we can and cannot say. Not by you, not by anybody. Not now, not ever. No matter how many flags you burn, no matter how many embassies you attack, free speech will prevail, and you'll suck it up and like it.

118

Peace in the Middle East

November 25, 2012

If we're serious about peace in the Middle East then we need to stop pretending that the Israelis are dealing with a rational enemy they can negotiate with, because, in doing that, we're helping to feed a massive political lie whose gravitational force has become so great it has warped reality.

It's Hamas who turned Gaza into a war zone recently, not Israel. And it's Hamas who will do so again, and again, and again. They don't care about the people there. They regard them as expendable in the cause of jihad. Why do you think there are no bomb shelters in Gaza, except, of course, for the brave Hamas fighters, who keep telling us they love death more than we love life, yet who scuttle away to safety as soon as the bombs come in, leaving the women and children to fend for themselves?

Wouldn't you suppose, as they were lobbing rockets over the border every day, that they would have given some thought to protecting ordinary people from possible retaliation? No. They'd rather build luxury hotels to accommodate gullible western journalists who can be trusted to portray them as heroic victims and the Israelis as neo-Nazi oppressors. In fact, it's Hamas who are the Nazis. Their political agenda is virtually identical, with the same genocidal supremacist delusions, and the same irrational violent hatred of Jews for being Jews. (Actually, the Nazis have the moral edge on Hamas. They were psychotic murdering scumbags as well, but at least they didn't use their own people as human shields.)

Hamas don't give a damn about the people of Gaza. They want them to be killed. Especially the children, whose bodies make wonderful propaganda. That's why they deliberately put them in the firing line, as fodder; as just another weapon to be used and discarded – or "martyred", which is the Islamic euphemism for somebody whose life has been thrown away for absolutely nothing.

Israel wants peace, and has always wanted peace. It's a modern civilised country and a world technological leader. The last thing it needs is war. That should be obvious to everyone. Israel would like nothing better than for Gaza to be thriving and prosperous and the people to be happy and free. They would even bankroll it if they thought it would work. But Hamas don't want the people happy and free. They want them miserable and blaming Jews for it, because Hamas are Islamic fanatics, jihadis, the same mentality that flew into the Twin Towers, and then blamed, guess who – the Jews.

They bribed the people of Gaza to elect them on a political platform, but once in power enforced their religion with an iron fist. Does anyone seriously think they would be elected again?

We'll never know because, once elected, an Islamist government is elected forever. And anybody who wants to argue about it can expect to be murdered and their corpse dragged through the streets behind a motorcycle, as happened last week in Gaza. These are men who are so hypnotised by their callous and violent religion, so bereft of any semblance of moral decency or compassion, that they'll happily murder someone for expressing a moment of joy by singing at a wedding, as happened last week in Gaza. Singing is outlawed in their Islamic paradise. Joy is forbidden. Happiness is haram.

They invoke the Koran in their founding charter, especially the passage about killing Jews; that's a big favourite. And they teach their children that the highest thing they can aspire to is to kill themselves by killing Jews. And these are the people the Israelis are supposed to negotiate with? It would be easier to reason with a rattlesnake.

So let's say you're the Israeli prime minister. What do you do? How do you deal with people who want you and everybody like you dead at any price, and whose position is not negotiable? Give up territory? Dismantle settlements? That's been tried. It doesn't work. Or didn't anybody notice? Israel dismantled settlements and uprooted thousands of people when it withdrew from Gaza, and what did it get? A barrage of bombs and rockets that hasn't stopped to this day.

So, clearly, dismantling settlements doesn't work. What else have we got? Mediation? Diplomacy? Restart the peace process? Yeah, in your dreams. There is no peace process, and there never will be as long as Hamas is around, because there is no such thing as a one-sided coin.

Hamas have made it clear that they have no intention of negotiating peace, ever. It's written right into their charter. Look it up. Peace would be un-Islamic. No negotiation and no let up in jihad (also enshrined in the charter) until every Jew in the Middle East has been driven out or killed. That's what they want, and it's not negotiable. Why do we keep pretending that they want something else?

The charter also forbids anybody else negotiating peace. So if peace ever does break out we can be sure Hamas will put a stop to it in double quick time.

But let's ignore all that and pretend it's about territory and politics and have another round of negotiations anyway. Let's hammer out another worthless accord. Let's get around a table and go through the motions again, and then hand out Nobel Prizes all round. We've got to be seen to be doing something, even if it's nothing.

And nothing is what it will be in spades, because negotiating with the likes of Hamas is like pouring light into a black hole. They don't want peace at any price. They want Jewish blood. End of story. That's why they break every ceasefire. That's why their own people are expendable. That's why no agreement with them is worth the paper it's written on. That's why there is no two-state solution and never will be as long as they're around. And that's why they need to be defeated decisively and permanently, or this madness will never, ever stop.

Shaking off these fanatical violent barbarians is the only way the Palestinian people will ever be truly liberated, and if the rest of us really care about peace, we should be honest enough to admit that.

4991437R00162

Printed in Great Britain
by Amazon.co.uk, Ltd.,
Marston Gate.